Southern Quilts

Celebrating Traditions, History, and Designs

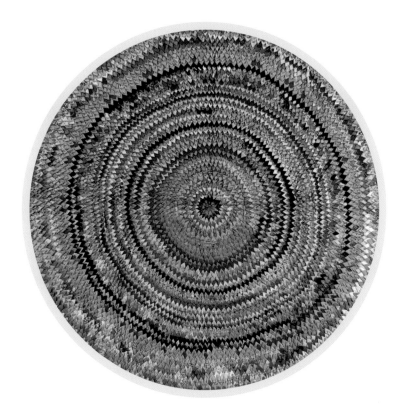

Schiffer Publishing Ltd.®

4880 Lower Valley Road • Atglen, PA 19310

Mary W. Kerr
Foreword by **Laurel Horton**

Other Schiffer Books by the Author:
Twisted: Modern Quilts with a Vintage Twist, ISBN 978-0-7643-5170-9
Recycled Hexie Quilts: Using Vintage Hexagons in Today's Quilts,
   ISBN 978-0-7643-4820-4
Dare to Dance: An Art Quilt Challenge, ISBN 978-0-7643-4612-5

Other Schiffer Books on Related Subjects:
100 Southern Artists, E. Ashley Rooney with Paula Allen,
   ISBN 978-0-7643-4241-7
Inspired by the National Parks: Their Landscapes and Wildlife in Fabric Perspectives,
   Donna Marcinkowski DeSoto, ISBN 978-0-7643-5119-8
Quilts Presidential and Patriotic, Sue Reich, ISBN 978-0-7643-5041-2

Proceeds from this project benefit the American Quilt Study Group.

Designed by RoS
Cover design by Molly Shields
Type set in Caecilia LT Std

ISBN: 978-0-7643-5502-8
Printed in China

Published by Schiffer Publishing, Ltd.
4880 Lower Valley Road
Atglen, PA 19310
Phone: (610) 593-1777; Fax: (610) 593-2002
E-mail: Info@schifferbooks.com
Web: www.schifferbooks.com

For our complete selection of fine books on this and related subjects, please visit our website at www.schifferbooks.com. You may also write for a free catalog.

Schiffer Publishing's titles are available at special discounts for bulk purchases for sales promotions or premiums. Special editions, including personalized covers, corporate imprints, and excerpts, can be created in large quantities for special needs. For more information, contact the publisher.

We are always looking for people to write books on new and related subjects. If you have an idea for a book, please contact us at proposals@schifferbooks.com.

To strong Southern women everywhere . . .

Thank you for your can-do spirit and welcoming
hearts. Your beauty, charm, grit, and grace
have paved the way for all of us,
regardless of where we may
choose to call home.

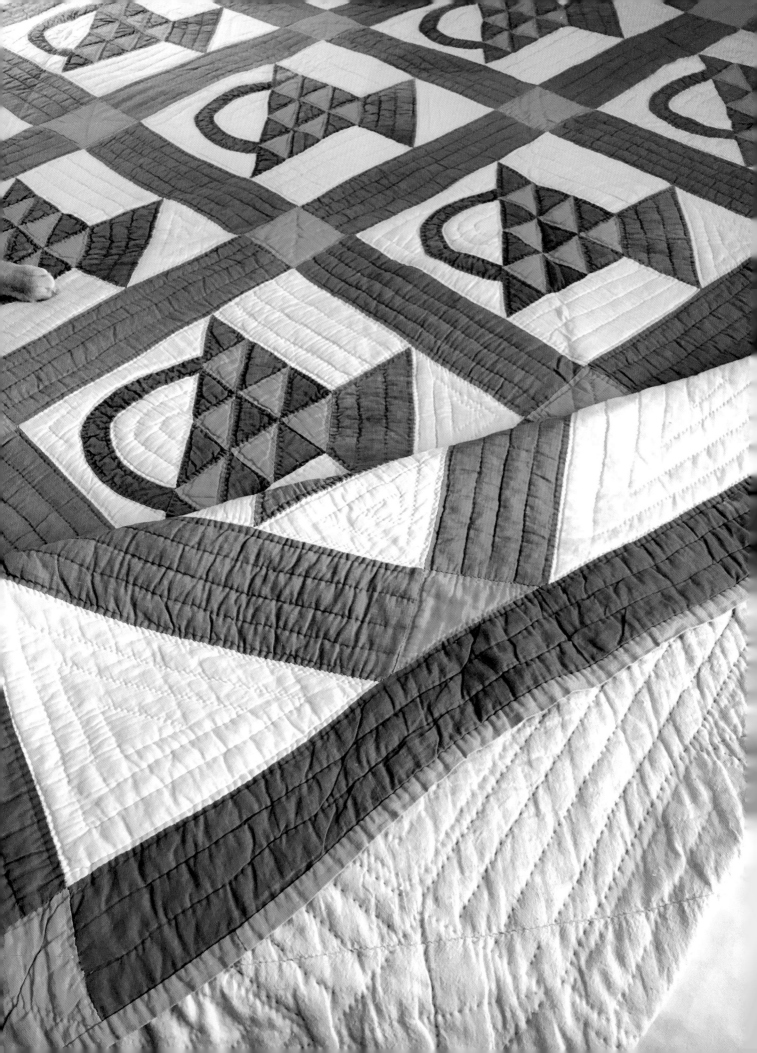

Contents

Baskets, circa 1870, 70" x 86".
North Carolina, maker unknown.
From a private collection.

Foreword
Southern Roots, Southern Patterns

The quilts compiled here offer a sampling of the rich variety and vitality of Southern patchwork. The patterns and colors reflect the influence of multiple cultural traditions brought into the region through nearly four centuries. Each quilt is the result of the choices made from among the styles, patterns, and fabrics available to the maker.

The earliest patchwork quilts in the Southern colonies came from traditions in the British Isles, including all-over hexagons and smallish square blocks of simple geometric divisions. During the early nineteenth century, a new style of patchwork patterns emerged from the confluence of German, English, and other European settlements in the Delaware River Valley, and the style spread rapidly in all directions. Around the same time, New England textile mills produced fabrics from Southern-grown cotton, and these products soon appeared on the shelves of general stores throughout the country. Southern women readily adopted the new larger block patterns and the bright, colorful fabrics for both their pieced and appliqué quilts.

The period from the 1840s to the turn of the twentieth century is often cited as the "Golden Age" of American quiltmaking. Southern quilts proliferated in number and variety, as women explored new combinations of colors and patterns. The rapid development of the Southern textile industry at the end of the nineteenth century resulted in the wide availability of inexpensive fabrics. Surviving utility quilts from the early twentieth century are characterized by the use of sewing scraps and factory mill ends, relatively simple patchwork patterns, heavy cotton battings, and large quilting stitches.

In the twentieth century, women's magazines promoted quiltmaking as the quintessential American craft. Patterns, both old favorites and newly designed, were available by mail order. In contrast, however, Southern quilt makers, black and white, seemed content to make quilts as their mothers and grandmothers had done. Women shared patterns with their relatives and their neighbors, by tracing the design from a finished quilt, or drawing it from memory. They reproduced original patterns, or might reinterpret them, intentionally or not. Some women created quilts with images inspired by their gardens or their dreams.

Over time, some special quilts remained in family homes, unfolded on special occasions and laid out on a bed. Others were carried to new homes and copied by new neighbors. Some Southern patterns remain associated with specific regions, while others became more widely known. This book exists because each of the contributors became intrigued by a particular, distinctive pattern, documented examples and variations, and compiled the results. The full range of Southern quilts cannot be encompassed by a single book. But perhaps the quilts, patterns, and stories collected here will encourage further efforts to identity and document the distinctive regional features that compose the complex character of American quiltmaking.

—Laurel Horton

Detail of Broken Star (page 89).
From the collection of Teddy Pruett.

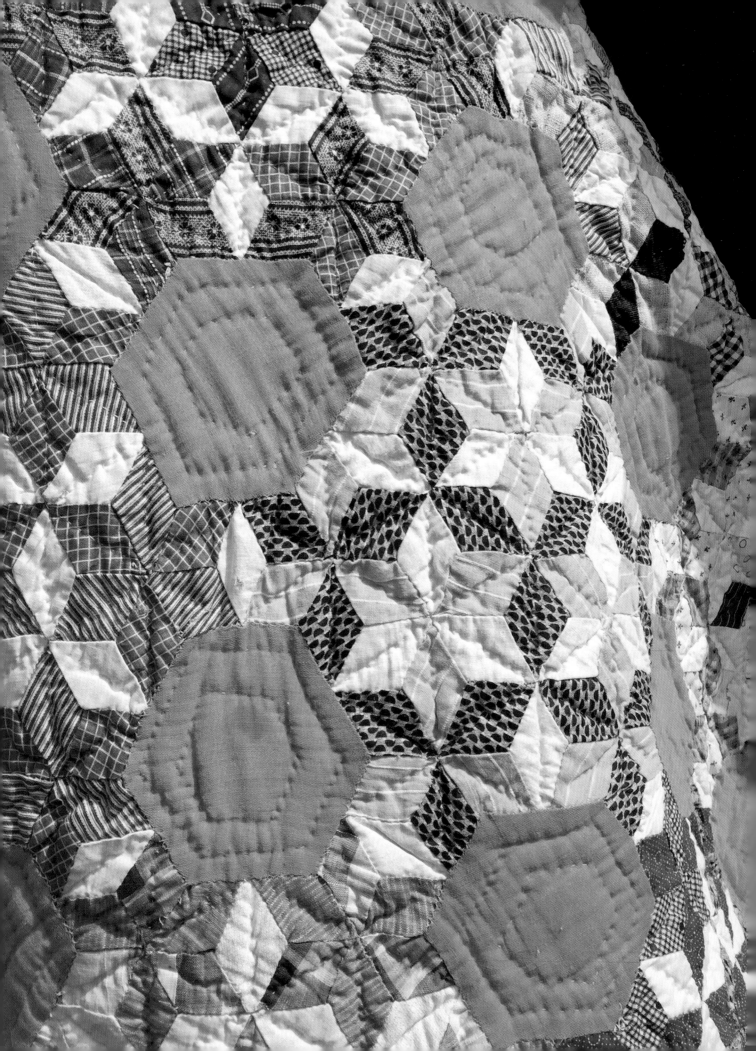

Acknowledgments

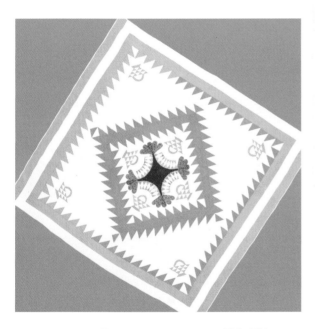

Whig's Defeat Basket Variation, circa 1920, 76" × 76". South Georgia, maker unknown. The center Whig's Defeat square dates to the 1860s with fugitive purple and period prints. Baskets were added in the 1920s to create this charming one-of-a-kind quilt. *From the collection of Mary Kerr.*

Thank you to this group of generous historians who worked with me on this project. I thank them for their willingness to share their research, enthusiasm, and vast knowledge. Their words and perspectives reflect the many ways we are able to find new opportunities to celebrate our quilting heritage. This manuscript was never intended to replicate the many historical pieces written about our heritage but rather a celebration of the many unique Southern quilt patterns.

With the exception of one, all of these writers are women of Southern heritage . . . dynamic individuals who were able to examine our quilting traditions in the context of our sometimes chaotic heritage. Their ingrained values give these women a genuine voice of understanding, pride, and acceptance. I am proud of our Southern heritage and so very grateful to the many institutions and individuals who contributed to this project. We are sharing quilts from seventeen institutions and more than fifty individual collections.

Thank you to my editor, Sandra Korinchak, and the staff at Schiffer Publishing, Ltd., for their unending encouragement and support. Thank you to Laurie Moody and Barb Garrett for their help with studio photography. Thank you to my sister, Karen Mitchell, for reading the manuscript in progress and helping to organize my thoughts. And last, but not least, thank you to my family and to the women in my life who serve as my army of cheerleaders. Life would not be the same without you!

—Mary W. Kerr
www.marywkerr.com

Close-up of Seven Sisters (see pages 104–105). *From the collection of Teddy Pruett.*

Primitive Star, circa 1910, 75" × 85". This heavy make-do star is quilted with concentric rectangles and heavily patched. No provenance known. *From the collection of Mary Kerr.*

Wonky Squares, circa 1900, 72" × 76". This thick Southern quilt features several sizes of squares and the signature Baptist Fan or elbow quilting. Provenance unknown. *From the collection of Mary Kerr.*

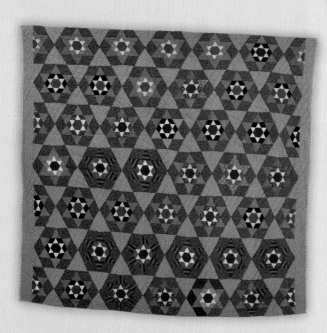

Hexagon Star, circa 1900, 78" × 90". This Hexagon Star variation was renamed the Ozark Star in 1935 by the *Kansas City Star*. Greensboro, Georgia, maker unknown. *From the collection of Mary Kerr.*

Whig's Defeat, circa 1870, 76" × 84". The intricate piecing of this pattern is paired with a pieced border on just two sides. Tennessee, maker unknown. *From the collection of Sharon Waddell.*

1

Making Do—A Southern Tradition
Mary W. Kerr

Southern quilts have a distinctive feel that sets them apart from other textiles. Many of these pieces are our heavy cotton quilts that are often finished with Baptist Fan or elbow quilting. These thick pieces are generally thought of as utilitarian pieces but many have simply been created using the available resources. Cotton was king throughout the South and the abundant crop was the primary batting used in the quilts of the region.

Southern women did not shy away from difficult patterns, and designs with multiple pieces were popular across the region. We can find basic patterns and finely finished pieces that showcase the needle skills prevalent throughout the South.

The established theme in quilts from every region of the South is that we made do with what we had or we went without. Across all socioeconomic situations, quilts from each region reflect the resources available. Those who lived along established trade routes had access to a wide range of fabrics while others were dependent upon their local mills. Textile mills were prevalent across the South from 1830 to 1960, and we see many of the remnants from these

mills in the quilts of the region. The plaid mills of the North Carolina Alamance region were first established in the 1850s and Georgia alone had 32 textile mills by the end of the 1940s. During the economic rebuilding after the Civil War, textiles took on an even greater significance as this industry provided jobs, goods, and economic development. Much has been written elsewhere about this industry and its fascinating history.

The theme of "make-do" has been present during every era of our Southern quiltmaking history. If you run out of fabric, use something else. If you need an extra border, add one. If you are short on skills or talent, make it work. Use up those leftover blocks as you mix, match, and create. This quirky attitude adds to the charm of our Southern pieces. I love the odd border, the use of a different block, and the often-unexpected pop of character! This was not an "I don't care what you think" mentality but a mind-set of making-do. It allowed Southern quilters to continue creating needed quilts and bedcoverings in times of hardship and economic downturn. Southern quilt makers were used to making do. It was a way of life that allowed our quilting traditions to survive.

Polka Dot Squares, circa 1900, 72" × 78". Note the quirky border treatment with two different sizes of squares and a complete disregard for starts and stops. Pace, Georgia, maker unknown. *From the collection of Mary Kerr.*

Feathered Star, circa 1890, 76" × 85". This pieced star is finely hand quilted in the Baptist Fan pattern with arcs that are ¼ inch apart. Notice the make-do border treatment. Central Tennessee, maker unknown. *From the collection of Mary Kerr.*

Tree of Paradise quilt top, circa 1910, 82" x 82". This hand pieced cotton top showcases the use of available fabrics in multiple colors and patterns. Provenance unknown. *From the collection of Sue Reich*

Summer Spread, circa 1920, 75" × 108". Circular blocks from the 1870s were paired with red shapes and machine appliquéd onto a denim sheet. Recycling at its finest! Front Royal, Virginia, maker unknown. *From the collection of Mary Kerr.*

Make-do quilt top with Whig's Defeat block in center surrounded by half square triangles. Circa 1890, 60" × 80". Cobb County, Georgia, maker unknown. *From the collection of Mary Kerr.*

Plaid Barrister's Block with a zig-zag setting, circa 1915, 78" × 104". Notice the great use of plaid fabrics and the unusual border treatments that extend the design. It has been quilted in straight lines and bound by machine. Central Tennessee, maker unknown. *From the collection of Mary Kerr.*

Oak Leaf, circa 1870, 74" x 79". Sampson County, North Carolina. *From the collection of the International Quilt Study Center, University of Nebraska–Lincoln, (2014.049.0001).*

Monkey Wrench Variation, circa 1880, 68" x 72". This quilt maker chose to be free-spirited with both her fabric choices and block placement. Unknown provenance. *From the collection of Sandra Starley.*

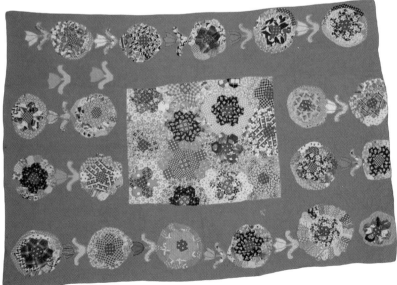

Make-do Floral Variation, circa 1940, 68" x 80". Leftover Grandmother's Flower Garden blocks were repurposed into this unique and amusing floral variation. Provenance unknown. *From the collection of Teddy Pruett* who calls this quilt *Grandma's Soccer Balls.*

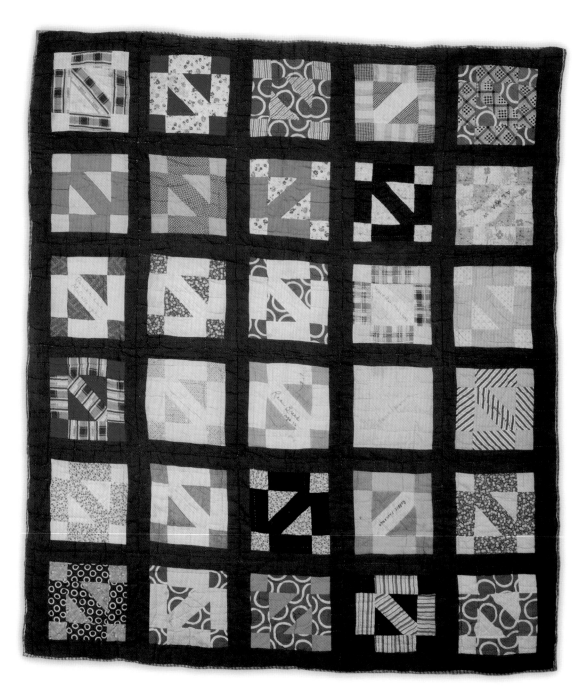

Alabama Signature quilt, circa 1935, hand and machine pieced, hand embroidered, hand quilted. This signature quilt was made in Roanoke, Alabama (Randolph County). The central block reads, "Resa Breed 16." According to the 1930 Census record, Resa's father, Cartie Breed, was a quiller in a cotton mill and her brother was a weaver in the mill. Other names inscribed on the quilt also had relatives who worked in the cotton mill. Robbie Faulkner, signer on the quilt, was a twister in the mill.
As published in *Quiltings, Frolicks, and Bees*, page 69. *From the collection of Sue Reich.*

Dresden Crazy Quilt, circa 1900, 68" × 69" without the
ruffle. Dresden plate blocks were combined with crazy quilt
blocks to create this decorative throw. No quilting with a
finished ruffled edge. Eastern Tennessee, maker unknown.
From the collection of Mary Kerr.

Petals (alternatively, Target), circa 1930–1940. 76" × 68". This quilt is from the estate of Lou Smith, Millport (Lamar County), Alabama. *From the collection of the International Quilt Study Center and Museum, University of Nebraska–Lincoln, Robert and Helen Cargo Collection, (2000.004.0114).*

2

Alabama Pine Burr
Mary Elizabeth Johnson

From the expansive vista of the sky in different seasons, to the compelling silhouettes of mountain ranges, to the birds of the air and the creatures of the earth and water, natural and planted gardens, and vast woodlands, American quilters have traditionally turned to nature for inspiration. In designs both realistic and abstract, quilters have pulled from their natural surroundings to fashion quilts of charm and beauty. The rich and varied plant life of the southeastern United States has motivated Southern quilters throughout centuries.

Surprisingly, it is not always the blossom or the leaf of a plant that is the stimulus for a compelling quilt design. In this pattern, it was the seed case of the plant that drew the attention of an erstwhile designer. As many animals of the forest know, those wood-like spikes that spiral around a core on a pine cone are protecting small nuts. Many cones grown on the various species of Southern pine trees feature sharply pointed spikes, which become the key component of the Pine Burr.

Pine Burr and Pine Cone are used interchangeably as names for this quilt design. Other names are Petal, Target, Cockleburr, and Bull's Eye. The final name is perhaps most appropriate for those quilts in which a single motif makes up the entire quilt top. Alabama quilter and National Heritage Fellow Nora Ezell named the thirty-block Pine Burr she made in 1959 (see page 22) her *Once in a Lifetime* quilt, because, as she explained, that is how often a person would make one. (See *My Quilts and Me: The Diary of an American Quilter*, by Nora Ezell, pages 25 and 28. Black Belt Press [now River City Press]: Montgomery, Alabama, 1999.)

To truly understand how the quilt design got its name, you must look at an actual pine cone in a certain way. Turn the cone so you look directly at the base: you will see that

Set of 3 Pine Burr blocks, circa 1900, 11"–12" square. Hand stitched with wool, cotton, and challis. Provenance unknown. *From the collection of Mary Kerr.*

the spikes or scales spiral out from the center, where a stem had attached the cone to the tree. The spiraling continues to the tip of the cone. The effect is one of concentric overlapping rows of scales. Interpreted in fabric, each row of scales is done in a different color, either random or according to a predetermined color scheme.

Eminent African American quilt historian Cuesta Benberry said that the Pine Burr was popular among Southern African American quilters from the early to late twentieth century, and that Pine Burr was held in high esteem as a

Once in a Lifetime, by Nora Ezell, dated December 1959, 77" x 95". Mrs. Ezell had been quilting at least fifteen years when she made this quilt, and she still considered it a challenge. Eutaw (Greene County), Alabama. *From the collection of the International Quilt Study Center and Museum, University of Nebraska–Lincoln, Robert and Helen Cargo Collection, (2000.004.0027).*

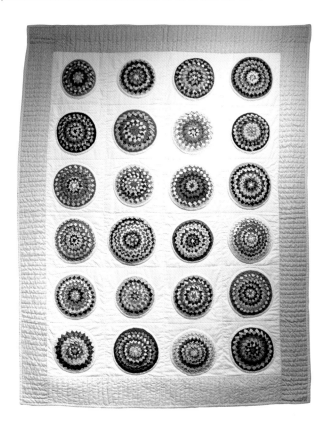

Pine Burr, by Loretta Pettway Bennett, 2001–2002, 60" × 77". This quilt was made by Loretta Pettway Bennett of Gee's Bend, Alabama. *From the collection of the Alabama Department of Archives & History.*

Pine Burr, also Petal, circa 1960–1970. 64" × 71". Tuscaloosa, Alabama, maker unknown. *From the collection of the Art Fund, Inc., at the Birmingham Museum of Art; gift of Helen and Robert Cargo. Accession #AFI.15.2007. Photograph by Seth Pathasema.*

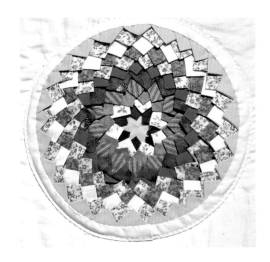

Detail of Pine Burr by Loretta Pettway Bennett

masterpiece work because of its difficulty of construction. Her assertion is coincidentally underlined in this chapter by the fact that all of the examples we feature were made by African Americans.

The difficulty of construction begins with the fact that circular quilt motifs are in general more complicated to execute than square or rectangular ones. That reality is compounded in this case by the fact that the Pine Burr is three-dimensional. This means that each of the hundreds of triangles making up the design must remain separate and independent of the others. In order to be successfully separate, each triangle must be finished on all sides—so there is no "right" and "wrong" side. The petals are placed so that the folded—therefore finished—corner of the tiny triangle points to the center of the circle, and the raw edges are on the outside of the circle. Each row of petals is stitched individually in place by hand as the layers are built up.

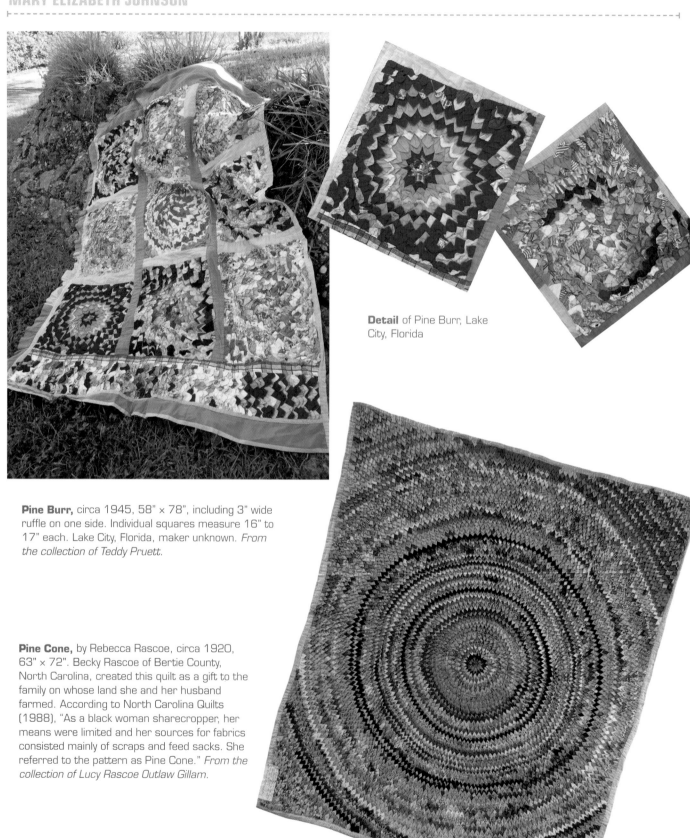

Detail of Pine Burr, Lake City, Florida

Pine Burr, circa 1945, 58" × 78", including 3" wide ruffle on one side. Individual squares measure 16" to 17" each. Lake City, Florida, maker unknown. *From the collection of Teddy Pruett.*

Pine Cone, by Rebecca Rascoe, circa 1920, 63" × 72". Becky Rascoe of Bertie County, North Carolina, created this quilt as a gift to the family on whose land she and her husband farmed. According to North Carolina Quilts (1988), "As a black woman sharecropper, her means were limited and her sources for fabrics consisted mainly of scraps and feed sacks. She referred to the pattern as Pine Cone." *From the collection of Lucy Rascoe Outlaw Gillam.*

Perhaps part of the reason for its universal appeal is the Pine Burr's representation of Alabama's forest products industry, which has been a mainstay of the economy, affecting the lives of many quilters, because it employs their husbands, sons, and brothers. The Pine Burr design was designated the official quilt of the state of Alabama by the legislature on March 11, 1997, with the following proclamation:

WHEREAS, THE FREEDOM QUILTING BEE WAS ORGANIZED AS AN OUTGROWTH OF THE CIVIL RIGHTS MOVEMENT IN 1966, ONE OF THE FEW ALL BLACK WOMEN'S COOPERATIVES IN THE COUNTRY; AND

WHEREAS, THE FREEDOM QUILTING BEE HAS ACHIEVED NATIONAL RECOGNITION FOR ITS QUILTS BY USING DESIGNS THAT COME FROM 140-YEAR-OLD TRADITION; AND

WHEREAS, CHINA GROVE MYLES, A FARMER, WAS THE ONLY ONE LEFT IN GEE'S BEND WHO COULD SEW THE PINE BURR QUILT, A PATTERN INVOLVING HUNDREDS OF TEDIOUS SWATCHES THAT UNFOLD BEFORE THE EYE IN A BREATHTAKING, THREE-DIMENSIONAL EFFECT; AND

WHEREAS, NETTIE YOUNG, ALSO A FARMER, IS THE ONLY WOMAN NOW WORKING AT THE BEE WHO WAS AMONG ITS ORIGINATORS, AND WHO TYPIFIES THE HISTORY OF THE BLACK RACE IN ALABAMA; AND

WHEREAS, QUILTS AND ARTIFACTS OF THE CIVIL RIGHTS ERA, WHICH WILL BE PRESENTED AND STORED IN THE FREEDOM QUILTING BEE, WILL PROVIDE AN ACCURATE DOCUMENTATION OF THE EVENTS TAKING PLACE IN AMERICAN HISTORY; AND

WHEREAS, A LOVE AND UNDERSTANDING OF THE HISTORY OF OUR STATE ARE ENHANCED BY TRADITIONS THAT HAVE BECOME A PART OF OUR WAY OF LIFE AND THE CUSTOMS OF THE AMERICAN PEOPLE, AND THE OFFICIAL RECOGNITION OF THE PINE BURR QUILT WILL INDEED ENHANCE THE CULTURAL STATURE OF ALABAMA BOTH NATIONALLY AND INTERNATIONALLY; NOW THEREFORE,

BE IT RESOLVED BY THE LEGISLATURE OF ALABAMA, BOTH HOUSES THEREOF CONCURRING, THAT IN RECOGNITION OF A MEANINGFUL SYMBOL FOR A STATE QUILT, THE PINE BURR QUILT IS HEREBY DESIGNATED AS THE OFFICIAL STATE QUILT OF ALABAMA.

BE IT FURTHER RESOLVED, THAT A COPY OF THIS RESOLUTION BE PRESENTED TO THE FREEDOM QUILTING BEE WITH SINCERE BEST WISHES FOR FUTURE SUCCESS.

APPROVED MARCH 11, 1997.

—*Acts of Alabama, No. 97-111*

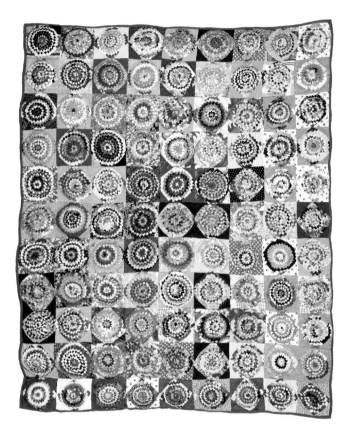

Pine Burr, 1974, 69" × 84". This masterpiece was created by an in-law of China Grove Myles, Gee's Bend, Alabama. *From the collection of the Birmingham Museum of Art, Birmingham, Alabama. Museum purchase with funds provided by the Fashion Group, Int., Birmingham. Accession # 1991.179. Photograph by Seth Pathasema.*

It is momentous that the Alabama state legislature has appointed one distinctive quilt design as the official state quilt, while simultaneously honoring the contribution of African American quilters to Alabama's cultural history.

3

Alamance Appliqué
Kathlyn Sullivan

Before the availability of good transportation, pockets of fairly isolated rural communities developed their own styles in the fields of art and architecture. One example of this is a rural, largely German-immigrant-populated community near the town of Gibsonville on the border of Eastern Guilford and Western Alamance Counties in the Piedmont area of North Carolina. A very distinct floral rose pattern became popular there, with most of its makers having ties to the local Brick German Reformed Church.

The majority of examples are made up of 6 large (20 to 25 inch) appliquéd blocks with pieced sashing and appliquéd borders on three sides. Occasionally a quilt had only one border. Perhaps that size was "big enough" for a bed next to a wall.

Most of the quilts had simple triple sashing with 9 patch corners, although 7 strips sashing with 49 patch corners exist. While settings vary, the rose appliqué itself is quite distinctive with a central scalloped 8 lobed flower with 6 leaves and a long upper stem with 3 buds at the top and a lower stem with leaves. From the base of the stem encompassing the flowers is a pair of large curved serrated leaves with similarly shaped lighter colored echoed centers. These serrated leaves are similar to another popular German-American favored pattern, the Princess Feather. The block motif sits at a corner-to-corner angle but is set square in the quilts. One family in the area referred to the pattern as American Beauty Rose. Another maker decided that they would substitute a tulip flower, another favored German-American pattern.

Fabric choices were limited for Southern quilt makers. The source of fabric was primarily the crossroads general store. The growth of the textile mills and the completion of rail transportation systems eventually made more goods available at competitive prices. Southern mills produced plain cloth dyed as a solid. Unbleached domestic, often referred to as homespun, was the least expensive cloth and is seen almost universally as the backing choice for Southern quilts. Printed cloth was not produced locally until just before the start of the twentieth century; until that time prints were imported from Northern mills, which made them more expensive.

When it came to quilt pattern, color, and designs, the German-American quilt makers relied on their own cultural standards. Color choices were often vivid, even gaudy. Repetition, precision, and use of sashing was usual. Love of nature is evident in their floral designs.

Bibliography

Roberson, Ruth, ed. *North Carolina Quilts*. Chapel Hill, NC: The University of North Carolina Press, 1988.

Sullivan, Kathlyn F. *Gatherings: America's Quilt Heritage*. Paducah, KY: American Quilter's Society, 1995.

Unknown Rose Appliqué, circa 1875, 74" x 88". Created by Nancy Stafford Spoon Shoffner (1834–1906), Alamance County, North Carolina. This is one of two quilts of the same pattern by the maker but in different colors. *North Carolina Quilt Project, courtesy of the North Carolina Museum of History.*

Unknown Rose Appliqué Quilt, circa 1900, 67" × 79". Created by Sarah Elizabeth (Betty) Friddle Smith (1862–1937), Eastern Guilford County, North Carolina. Note the single border. *From the collection of Vicki Burleson.*

Unknown Rose Appliqué, circa 1890, 69" × 86". Created by Minerva E. Sharpe Isley (1857–1941), Alamance County, North Carolina. Note fugitive dyes turning from green to brown and polka dot cloth background. *From the collection of Janice D. Pope.*

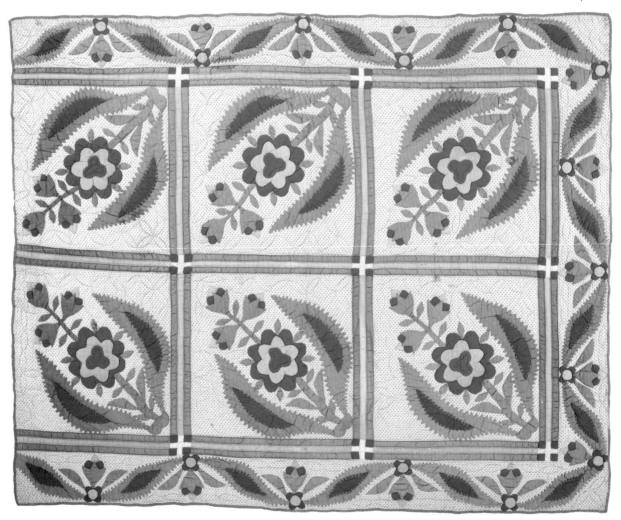

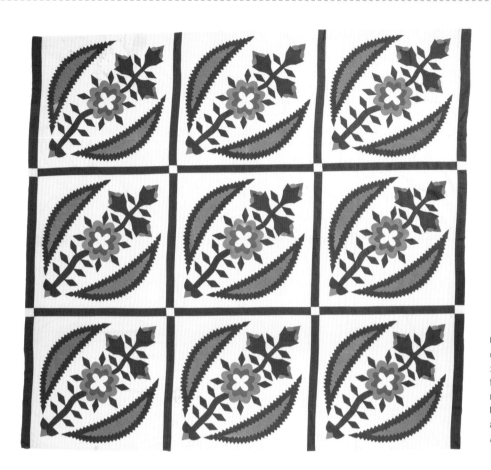

One of a pair of appliqué quilt tops, circa 1880, 79" x 84". This pair of tops was found at a country auction near Gibsonville, North Carolina. The maker's appliqué skills are the best. *From a private collection.*

Unknown Rose Appliqué Quilt, circa 1890, by Mary May Neese. Note appliquéd elements on the sashing and serrated leaves along the single border. *North Carolina Museum of History.*

Unnamed Appliqué Quilt, circa 1870, unknown maker from Gaston County, North Carolina. Nine red blocks are in a frame-like set with added strips in the top and bottom borders to extend length. *Collection of Kathleen Metelica Cray.*

Single block from Gaston County, North Carolina.

4

Appliqué Medallion
Kathlyn Sullivan

What does a 1749 cupboard from Baden, Germany in the Karlsruhe Badisches Landesmuseum have to do with quilts in North and South Carolina? Perhaps a great deal. Quilt documentation projects uncovered many unique pattern quilts originating in Piedmont North and South Carolina, the very areas settled by ethnic Germans.

The German population was a small fraction of the entire population of the area. They came seeking good land in the latter half of the eighteenth century, settled by the time of the Revolution. Most arrived at the port of Philadelphia and traveled the Old Wagon Road through Lancaster, York, and down the Shenandoah Valley of Virginia. Much of the land was already taken in Virginia and hostility with the Indian population motivated them to continue on. Many stopped in North Carolina, others continued down through Salisbury and Charlotte into Piedmont South Carolina into an area known as Dutch Fork.

By adhering to their language, and their churches not gaining converts, the Germans remained a very closed group. After 1790 there were few newcomers. The nineteenth century German immigrants settled in the cities of the Midwest.

There is little evidence that North and South Carolinians of German lineage were involved with quiltmaking before 1850. Looms and weaving were part of their culture. By 1850 the language barriers were breaking and the Germans intermingled with the majority Scots-Irish population and were exposed to their quiltmaking traditions and quilting bees.

Appliqué block quilts cut into medallion shapes were discovered during the North Carolina quilt documentation days. The cloth was carefully folded and cut out much like a paper snowflake with eight lobes. The cutouts were then

Line drawing of painted cupboard from Bonndorf, Baden, Germany, 1749. *From the collection of Badisches Landesmuseum, Karlsruhe.*

opened up and appliquéd to a base fabric. They were primarily unnamed graphic quilts and the unusual medallion-like blocks sparked interest in their origin. Alternating two color variations of the medallion means that two cut medallions, one of each color, were dissected and re-sewn together.

The Baden cupboard shown on page 31 has twin medallions painted on it with twelve lobes each—the very design found on the quilts although the quilts were most likely to have eight lobes. Finally, here is a positive connection to German folk art adapted to cloth. This explains why the majority of these quilts were in a German style.

Only one family mentioned that the pattern was called Wonder of the World. Another suggested Sun Wheel. The

Unnamed Appliqué Quilt top without borders, circa 1850. Unknown provenance. Photographed in Paducah, Kentucky, cemetery by Mary Kerr. *From the collection of Cindy Rennells.*

Single block from Rennells quilt top

Unnamed Appliqué Quilt with swag border, circa 1850, 96" × 96". This quilt is attributed to the Shoffner Family, Western Alamance County, North Carolina. The quilting thread matches the appliqué pieces. Quilted hearts may signify that it was made as a wedding quilt. *From a private collection.*

majority of the quilts were attributed to makers who were claimed as being of German extraction and members of the Lutheran or German Reformed Churches. The pattern was shared however, with neighbors. An old boatman on the Yadkin River recollected his mother sending the pattern with him to deliver to friends down river.

Jan Murphy's study of this pattern and many examples added later, found that the quilts were about evenly divided between one piece and alternating color medallions. Most had two curved sewn slits at the top of each lobe. About half have serrated rather than smooth top edges and nearly all have serrated internal edges. The medallion centers vary and only pre–Civil War examples have additional floral appliqués or swag borders. The

earliest quilts tend to have matching thread used in the quilting on each color motif. One variation quilt had cut out hearts in every other lobe. Another made use of cut lobes to create a flower bloom appliqué in what appears to be a tulip base.

We are fortunate that many of these Medallion quilts were saved and treasured. Many pieced quilts were simply used up or found their way to the tobacco barn when workers spent twenty-four hours a day keeping the fires going to cure the crop. Other old quilts covered wagons of tobacco leaves heading to the market houses. Appliqué quilts were often referred to as the best, and were never or infrequently used but saved to make the house attractive for company or for Sunday visitors.

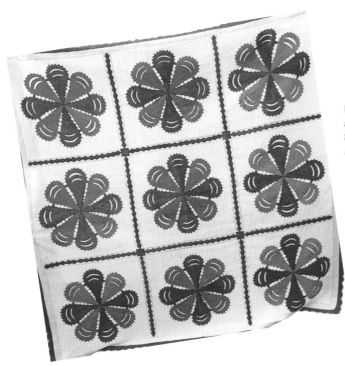

Unnamed Appliqué Quilt with appliquéd sashing, circa 1850, 89" × 89". Unknown provenance. *From the collection of Jean Lury.*

Bibliography

Horton, Laurel. "Textile Traditions in South Carolina's Dutch Fork." In *Bits and Pieces Textile Traditions*, edited by Jeannette Lasansky, 72–79. Union, SC: Oral Traditions Project of the Union County Historical Society, 1991.

Murphy, Jan. "Design Influences on an Unnamed Regional Pattern." In *Uncoverings 1987*, edited by Laurel Horton and Sally Garoutte, 41–55. San Francisco: American Quilt Study Group, 1989.

Ritz, Gislina. *Alte bemalte Bauernmobel Europa.* Munich: Verlag Georg D W Callwey, 1970.

Roberson, Ruth, ed. *North Carolina Quilts.* Chapel Hill, NC: The University of North Carolina Press, 1988.

Sullivan, Kathlyn. "The Legacy of German Quiltmaking in North Carolina." *In Bits and Pieces Textile Traditions,* edited by Jeannette Lasansky, 64–71. Union, SC: Oral Traditions Project of the Union County Historical Society, 1991.

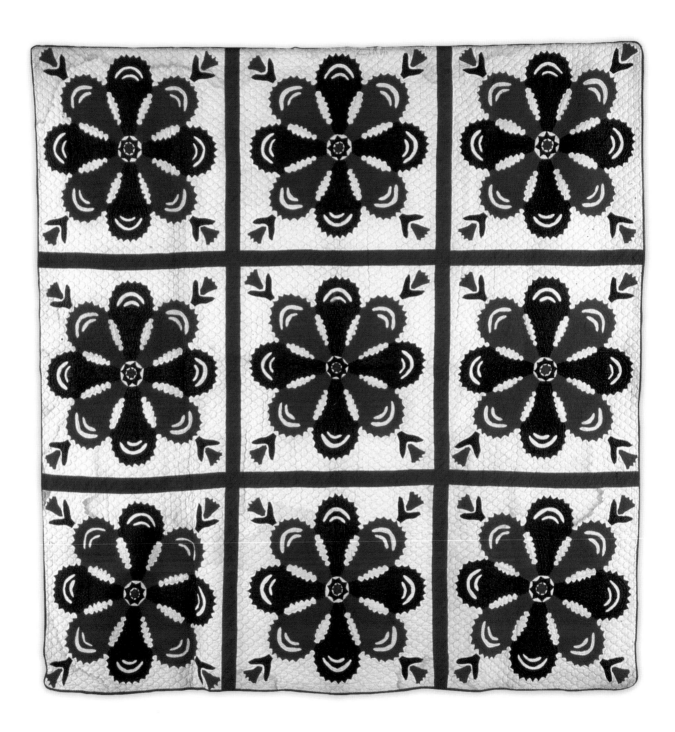

Unidentified Appliqué Quilt, signed and dated in embroidery, January 23, 1877, 86" x 86", Emma Poovey. The Lincoln County, North Carolina, quilt is a two-color medallion with tulip flowers and fancy block centers. It is unusual to see a North Carolina quilt from this time period without borders. *From a private collection.*

Unnamed Appliqué Quilt, circa 1875, 77" × 90", unknown maker, Mecklenburg County, North Carolina. *From a private collection.*

Unnamed Appliqué Quilt, circa 1860, 90" x 94". This quilt was passed down from the Watkins family to Mr. Bailey Looper of Pelzer, South Carolina. Note the unusual use of print fabrics to create the medallions. *From the collection of Abigail Dolinger.*

Detail of Watkins quilt

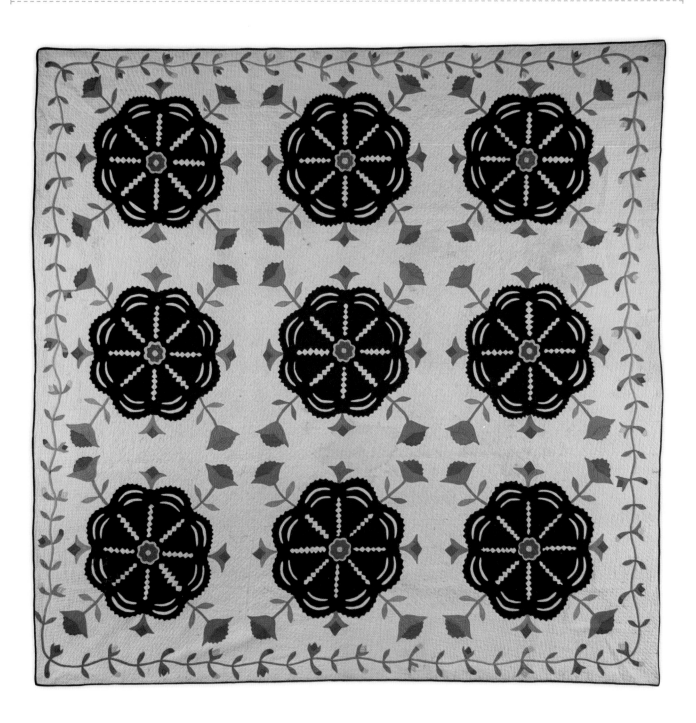

Unnamed Appliqué Quilt with floral elements, circa 1850. This quilt was made by a member of the Gaither Family in Iredell County, North Carolina. Contains embroidered initials DAHG. Superior workmanship and design techniques. Note the centers, the delicate vine border, and the additional floral elements. Gregg Museum of Art & Design, Gift of Louise and Banks Talley, Jr., in honor of their ancestors in the Talley, Gaither, Wooten, Dillon, and Trotter families. *Photo by Matthew Gay.*

5

Circles and Spikes
Teddy Pruett

Star in a Circle, circa 1930. 68" × 76". Large pieced blocks are quilted over a thick batt with Baptist Fan quilting. Notice the wavy sashing and the inconsistency of piecing. This has a homespun back that is turned back to front. Eastern Tennessee, maker unknown. *From the collection of Mary Kerr.*

Detail of Star in a Circle

We know a lot about Southern quilts, "we" being historians, researchers, appraisers, collectors, and admirers. We also don't know a lot about Southern quilts. Take, for instance, quilts made with circular designs. Years of observation confirm that quilt makers in the deep South were extremely fond of circular patterns, particularly circular patterns with points, teeth, and spikes. Although these same patterns may show up in the North, the numbers are small compared to the great numbers made in the South. It would be gratifying to know why this is so, but the answer to that question is not readily available.

When observing collectible antique or vintage items such as coins, baseball cards, or even cars, there is no question about when, where, what, and how much. These items were mass produced; there are records, guides, trails to follow that will tell us everything about the item in question. Quilts, being individual creations, don't have that sweet, easy path backward that tells us everything we want to know. In a perfect world, each quilt would be labelled with all pertinent information, but that isn't reality. A step down from perfection, yet still quite desirable, would be diary entries or letters describing the quilts people were making, complete with the name of the pattern and a mention of the pattern's source. Unfortunately, the rare diary entry usually alludes to "my patchwork" or "quilted today" without elaboration. A quilt does, however, leave hints about the quilter's life. It tells a tale left by threads connecting us to the culture that produced it.

In extensive areas of the South, the predominant culture was that of the Scots Irish, or Ulster Scots. If you compare a quilt made by a member of this group with, for instance, a quilt by a quilt maker of Germanic heritage, also present

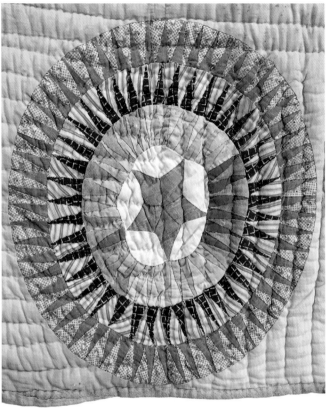

Sunburst Quilt, circa 1930. This quilt exhibits many of the characteristics of quilts from the Deep South. Hand-dyed sack/bag fabrics, feedsack bits, backing turned to front as opposed to binding, dyed bags for the backing, awkward workmanship, and odd color placement. And yet, this is an amazing master work. *From the collection of Teddy Pruett.*

Detail of Sunburst block

in areas of the South, the differences are pronounced. Quilters of the past observed their surroundings, they replicated what had been done before, they learned from their elders and continued tradition without being aware they were doing so. One woman related she was away at college before she learned there was an alternative to fan quilting.

These circular patterns are not for the faint of heart. Curved forms and long points, having bias edges, are difficult to work with and difficult to control. It would seem that only the most skilled piecer would take on such a challenge, but the plot thickens. A great number of Southern quilt makers, postbellum, particularly those of Scots Irish background, are known for less than perfect workmanship. Casual, crude, and haphazard are words that have been used to describe the work. So, this begs the question: Why would someone with less than stellar skills attempt the most difficult of patterns? One reason could be they were unaware their workmanship wasn't up to those arbitrary standards established by someone, somewhere; standards that had nothing to do with them. If every sashing you've ever seen wobbles slightly and fails to line up with the one above or below, it's probably okay that yours does as well. If points are lopped off here and there, if something is too large and ends up with a small

Pinwheel, circa 1890. Black and pink prints swirl on a homespun brown ground. Virginia Beach, Virginia, maker unknown. *From the collection of Teddy Pruett.*

String Pieced Circles, circa 1940. Circle blocks from the turn of the century were paired with bright red. The maker was short of blocks so she added a Mrs. Cleveland's Choice block in one corner! Southern make-do at its finest. *From the collection of Teddy Pruett.*

tuck, so what? Don't they all? The argument has been made that these less than perfect quilts were made in a rush to cover the family and provide warmth, but that theory is easily negated simply by observing the quilts closely. There are quilts here that are very obviously made to be "best" quilts, designed to knock your socks off, and they do. They are stunning works visually if not technically.

Quilters who were so fond of this pattern were most likely unaware that the pattern is based on time honored design principles. Unity that comes from repetition of a motif, the symmetry of the circle, the excitement of the spiked forms in combination with the curves, and oh, that color! If the colors repeat in each block, there is even more unity. But if those blocks use varied fabrics, if those blocks are scrappy—wow! What a payoff! The eye is invited to travel around the quilt, trying to match things up, looking for repeats, rewarded by sparks of delight here and there. There's no wonder the variations of the curved-spiked block were so popular.

An attempt to find the source and establish the popularity of these spiky, circular patterns is made more difficult due to the fact that most pattern names were assigned in the twentieth century and may or may not have any relationship at all to what the maker called her (or his) quilt. Nomenclature is never simple, so even if we had records of pattern names, it is highly possible the name means one thing in a particular location and yet another thing entirely somewhere else. Circle and spike pattern names include Rising Run, Circle Saw, Pyrotechnics, Suspension Bridge, Wheel of Fortune, Wagon Wheel, Fly Wheel, Circle Star, and multiple patterns named Sunburst. Did the quilt makers call their quilts by these names? It's unlikely, at least until after the twentieth century assignment of names in printed media.

We see them, we collect them, we admire them. Why were these difficult patterns so popular in the South? At this point, we don't really have an answer. What we know for certain is that they came from the heart and soul of the maker, and that may be all we need to understand.

Rising Sun, circa 1940. The use of simple blue sashing gives the eye a place to rest. Unknown provenance. *From the collection of Sharon Waddell.*

Circular blocks, circa 1890. These blocks were made by Katie Hester Harvell in Bladen County, North Carolina. *From the collection of Loleta Thornton Andrews.*

Unknown Medallion, circa 1860. This unique pattern was created by Anna E. Stutzman of Rhea County, Tennessee. It is similar to a Chips and Whetstone design with more elaborate piecing. *From the collection of James Tallent.*

Russian Sunflower, circa 1870. This finely made example is a wonderful collection of period prints set with the ever popular cheddar. South Alabama, unknown maker. *From the collection of Teddy Pruett.*

Detail of Russian Sunflower

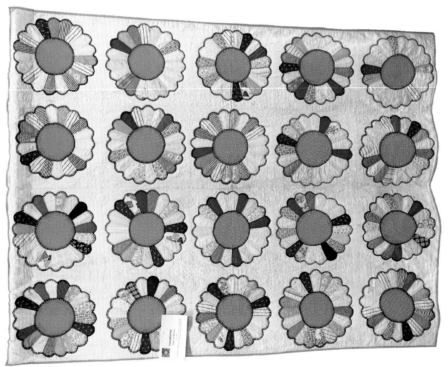

Dresden Plate, circa 1940, 68" × 89". Sometimes a quilter just chooses to create on a larger scale. This well-loved quilt features hand stitched buttonhole embroidery in black thread. Paducah, Kentucky, maker unknown. *From the collection of Mary Kerr.*

Cottage Tulip Signature Quilt, circa 1935, 58" × 81". The Cottage Tulip pattern was published by three different designers in the second quarter of the twentieth century; Evelyn Brown, *Kansas City Star*, and Carrie Hall. This design is rarely found as a signature quilt. The signers of this quilt were all farmers' wives from Colville, Arkansas.

As published in *Quiltings, Frolicks, and Bees*, page 64. *From the collection of Sue Reich.*

Detail of a Signature block

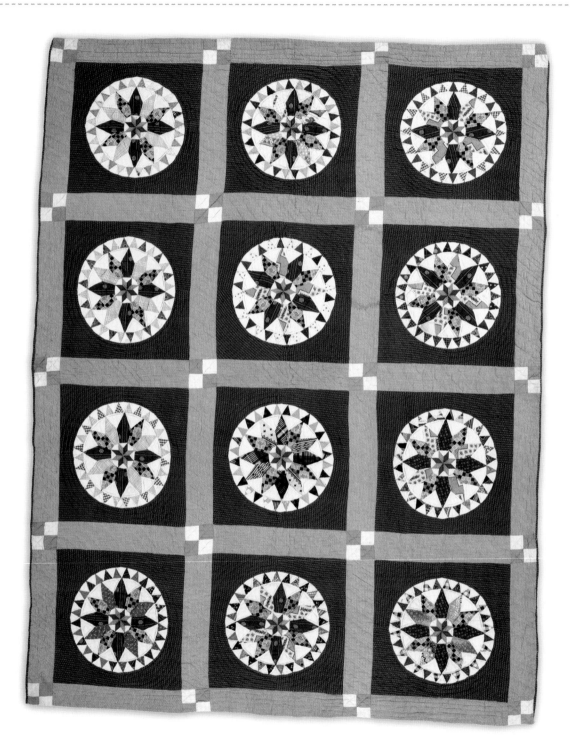

Compass Star, circa 1870, 71" × 92". This exquisite quilt showcases the many period prints that were available in the 1870s. The quilt appears to have never been used. It was purchased from a Commerce, Georgia, estate, maker unknown. *From the collection of Mary Kerr.*

Circle Saw top, circa 1930, 78" × 96". This hand pieced top includes plaids, checks, and feedsacks. It was called multiple names to include, Rising Sun, Wagon Wheel, Fly Wheel, Circle Saw, Wheel of Life, and the Wheel of Fortune. Liberty County, Georgia, maker unknown. *From the collection of Mary Kerr.*

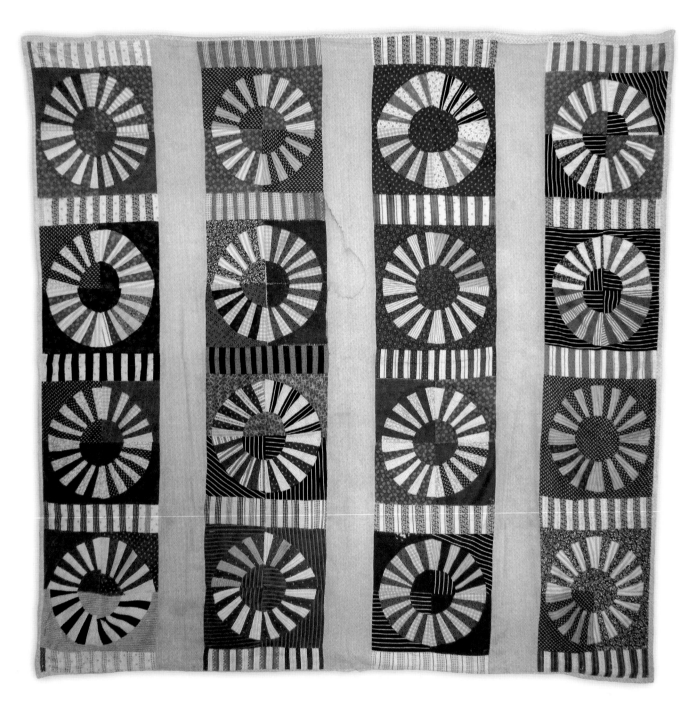

Wagon Wheel, circa 1890. The sashing on this quilt is
disintegrating but the blocks are still bright and strong.
It was created in Comfort, Texas, maker unknown. *From
the collection of Kathleen Metelica Cray.*

Sunburst Quilt, circa 1980, Shenandoah Valley, Virginia. Three rings of pieced triangles in each block are striking against the indigo background in this quilt. Squares on point create borders on two sides. Quilting is worked in diagonal triple lines a quarter inch apart and separated by half inches. This pattern is very similar to the Farmer's Fancy designs that are prevalent in the Shenandoah Valley. *From the collection of Polly Mello.*

Fly Wheel, circa 1880. The double rodded Baptist Fan quilting really shows on this soothing color palette. This quilt was created in Pace, Georgia, maker unknown. *From the collection of Teddy Pruett.*

Sunburst, circa 1880, 73" × 80". This fabulous explosion of color exemplifies a fine Southern quilt. Circles and impossible spikes set with triple sashing and straight cut borders. Created in Hamlet, North Carolina, maker unknown. *From the collection of the International Quilt Study Center and Museum, University of Nebraska–Lincoln, (2014.049.0008).*

Wagon Wheels, circa 1900, 70" × 82". This scrappy version is a delight to those of us who love a quilt with lots of fabrics, colors, and movement. It is quilted with all over diagonal lines. Provenance is unknown. *From the collection of DL Miller.*

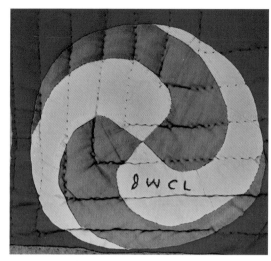

Close-up of Swirling Circle signature

Swirling Circles, circa 1870, 68" × 84". Swirling two color blocks are set with green sashing and yellow cornerstones. This piece has been quilted with a straight overall grid. There is a signature block in the lower right corner. Roanoke, Virginia, maker unknown. *From a private collection.*

Cotton Boll Quilt, circa 1875, 76" × 77".
This nine block quilt is attributed to the
Hinshaw Family of Randolph County, North
Carolina. *From a private collection.*

Cotton Boll
Kathlyn Sullivan

One of the most beloved and most graphic patterns from the South is the Cotton Boll. With the rise in periodicals and quilt documentation books in the late twentieth century, the Cotton Boll pattern saw resurgence in spite of the fact that it is a labor-intensive design. Most new and old patterns are done in bright red or oxblood and green on a white ground.

The earliest examples have pieced or appliquéd sashes and/or borders. One 1850s four-block example has a double swag border with floral buds and a pieced, embroidered, and appliquéd sashing. Another beauty in the North Carolina Museum of History has flying geese sashes and border with the addition of a floral appliqué in the corner blocks.

It would be interesting to know the specific origin of the quilt pattern. But we do have a few clues. In Greensboro stands Blandwood, the Italianate home of North Carolina Governor John Motley Morehead (1841–1845). In 1844 he had an addition built that was designed by Alexander Jackson Davis, a New York City architect who designed the state capitol building in Raleigh.

At Blandwood, the ceiling medallion and frieze designs around the walls at the ceiling were ancient designs from an early *Handbook of Ornament*, a staple reference for designers and architects. Davis would surely have a copy of this type of book. The akroter (a gable finish) and stele crest (a tombstone ornamentation) designs are surely related to what we know as Cotton Boll.

Morehead was the first governor of North Carolina to advocate for public education and education for women. He hosted many events in his home. Guests included many young women who were being educated in Greensboro. Could they have looked up and been inspired by the designs on the Blandwood ceiling (page 54)?

Cotton Boll quilts in the post–Civil War era were often plainer, with simple sashing and borders, and executed with less delicacy and precision. Many later examples were

Cotton Boll Quilt, circa 1850, 80" × 90". This four block quilt was created in Davie County, North Carolina, by Temperance Neely Smoot. Brown stains attributed to a leaky trunk when quilt was hidden from Union soldiers during the Civil War. *North Carolina Quilt Project, courtesy North Carolina Museum of History.*

Cotton Boll Quilt with pieced, appliquéd and embroidered sashing, and swag border, circa 1850, 81" x 82". This four block masterpiece was created in Iredell County, North Carolina, maker unknown. *From a private collection.*

Detail of the Iredell County quilt

Cotton Boll Quilt, circa 1920, 70" x 70". This four block quilt was created by Virginia Harrelson Bell (1878–1967). *Photo by the North Carolina Museum of History.*

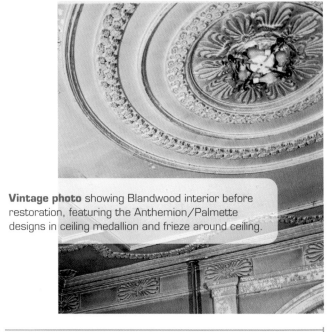

Vintage photo showing Blandwood interior before restoration, featuring the Anthemion/Palmette designs in ceiling medallion and frieze around ceiling.

also plagued by fugitive dyes, losing their color. A circa 1910 quilt has a simpler but related block with fewer elements and only one boll per block. It is also straight stitched, machine appliquéd, and has an overall unsophisticated quilting design. A 1920s example adds two additional colors to the bolls and has a heavy-handed setting.

Coming full circle, the 2005 North Carolina Quilt Symposium opportunity quilt was inspired by the 1850s Frances Johnston quilt in the North Carolina Museum of History. Robin Caruso made the adaptations and the Colonial Quilt Lovers Guild, the Greenville Quilt Guild, and the Pamlico River Quilt Guild collaborated to create a masterpiece (see page 56).

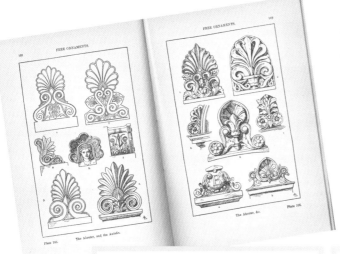

Pages of Anthemion designs found in the nineteenth-century design reference, *Handbook of Ornament.*

Bibliography

Meyer, Franz Sales. *A Handbook of Ornament.* New York: Architectural Book Publishing Company, n.d.

Roberson, Ruth, ed. *North Carolina Quilts.* Chapel Hill, NC: The University of North Carolina Press, 1988.

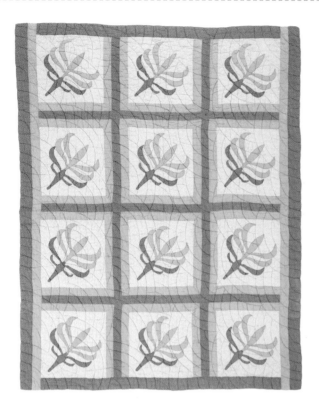

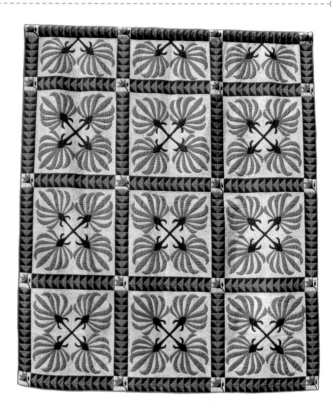

Cotton Boll Variation Quilt, circa 1900, 68" × 80". This simpler version features straight stitch machine appliqué and is hand quilted in fans. An "E" is embroidered on the back in white thread. The fugitive dye was originally red. This quilt was collected in Wytheville, Virginia, maker unknown. *From a private collection.*

Cotton Boll Quilt made for North Carolina Quilt Symposium by members of the Colonial Quilt Lovers Guild, Greenville Quilt Guild, and Pamlico River Guild, all Eastern North Carolina. Inspired by the Frances Johnston Cotton Boll Quilt in the North Carolina Museum of History with adaptations by Robin Caruso. *Collection of and photo by Neva Hart.*

Cotton Boll Quilt, circa 1930, 78" × 78". Notice the brighter color palette of the 1930s used to create this classic pattern. Provenance unknown. *From the collection of Mary Kerr.*

Cotton Boll Quilt, circa 1920, 72" × 73". This colorful variation was created by an unnamed woman who also made baskets from Randolph or Chatham County, North Carolina. *From the collection of the International Quilt Study Center, University of Nebraska–Lincoln, (2014.049.0019).*

Crown of Thorns, circa 1870, 87" × 103". This variation was made by Susan Fish McCallay in Troup County, Georgia. The quilter's attention to scale, the addition of the appliqué brown stars, and her use of a bright bold scheme makes her version of the pattern memorable. *From the collection of Merikay Waldvogel.*

7

Crown of Thorns
Merikay Waldvogel

Rocky Mountain, circa 1870, 78" × 100". Texas quilter Sarah Redmond added flower motifs inside the open areas formed by the traditional layout. *From the Volckening Collection, photo by Bill Volckening.*

Quilt historians in the South call this pattern Rocky Mountain or Crown of Thorns, but most people know it as "New York Beauty." What we all agree on is that it is one of the most exciting and memorable patterns ever designed. Who first came up with the design? That person's name is irretrievably lost to history, but she or he most likely lived in the South since many more of the earliest examples remain in the South today with original owners and in museum collections. Let's take a closer look at the pattern's origins, its variations, and that intriguing story of how it got its name.

It originated in the Southeast with examples coming from Alabama, Georgia, Mississippi, North Carolina, and Tennessee. A quilt in this pattern from Tennessee was dated in the quilting "1857." A quilt from Georgia was titled "Rocky Mountain" in the quilting. Some of the most striking examples are those pieced of the red, green, and yellow prints from the 1850s. In the late 1800s, solid green fabrics in the quilts fade to beige. The concentric arcs are sometimes pieced of the brown calico and double-pink prints that were so popular at that time. In the 1930s, when the name changed to New York Beauty, the traditional colors were replaced by Nile green, lavender, pink, and yellow.

The piecing required making units composed of hundreds of points on both straight and curved edges. Multi-pointed stars were inserted at the cross points and at the quilt corners. There were two layouts—one with a strong diagonal criss-crossing the surface and the other forming a boxed grid. The two layouts appear with equal frequency in quilts dating from the mid-nineteenth century. It's interesting to note that the quilt design that caused the name change in 1930 was the more dramatic X layout. In

Crown of Thorns, circa 1890, 71" x 77". Cocke County, Tennessee, maker unknown. Pieced of fabrics in white and red and green solids, this quilt shows how time and light can affect the design as the fabrics fade. The green in this quilt was originally a deeper, darker shade. This fading of green to a khaki or beige was commonly found in quilts made in the late 1800s. Notice also here the larger pieces and the less elaborate quilting. This pattern was beloved by all—newly minted quilters as well as the experts. *From the collection of Merikay Waldvogel.*

Detail of the Cocke County quilt

some, an appliquéd vine border replaced the spiky borders. Wide open areas behind the arched segments allowed for quilting both utilitarian and elaborate. These are quilts to enjoy from far away as well as up close.

The fact that the quilts were so striking meant they often received notice at quilt fairs, in magazines, and among families. In 1911, a woman from Illinois won the first prize of $10 in Comfort Club's Quilt Contest sponsored by *Pictorial Review*. The editors wrote: "This pattern is known as The Rocky Mountain. It was by far the handsomest quilt submitted in the contest from all points. The stitches were so small and so even that they looked almost like machine work. Yet every stitch was put in by hand, both in the piecing and quilting."

Prior to 1930, the published names for the pattern were Crown of Thorns, Morning Sun, Rocky Mountain, and Rocky Mountain Road. After Stearns & Foster Co. added it to its pattern line and called it "New York Beauty" the name caught on, even though few if any quilts in this pattern were made in New York State. By the 1980s, at quilt documentations, even in the South, families came in saying their quilt was a New York Beauty. Asked what other names

Close-up of quilting detail

Rocky Mountain, circa 1870, 68" × 82". An unnamed Georgia quilter stitched the words "Rocky Mountain" into the quilting design of this quilt. This quilt is an important historical document that confirms the use of the name Rocky Mountain for this pattern in the South in the late 1800s. *From the collection of Karen Downer.*

they called it, the name Rocky Mountain was the most commonly reported.

One can pinpoint the date when this nearly 100-year-old Southern quilt pattern became "New York Beauty." Fritz Hooker, sales manager at Stearns & Foster Co., manufacturers of quilt batting, came up with a gimmick to increase the sales of batting. His plan was to revamp the batting wrapper, making it colorful and attractive. He added quilt pattern blocks to the outside of the wrapper and included a free full-size pattern on the inside. It turned out to be not only a boon to quilt makers eager to "get quilting," but also a clever means of monitoring customers' interests. If a quilt maker did not like the free pattern, she could write to the company requesting another one in their pattern line.

Fritz Hooker, at first without an in-house designer to consult, went to his local public library to look for quilt pattern blocks. He also wanted antique quilts he might use. On one trip, he found a large four-block Princess Feather quilt and another quilt that eventually became "New York Beauty." Both quilts became part of the Mountain Mist Collection, which today is housed at the International Quilt Study Center and Museum at the University of Nebraska at Lincoln. On closer examination of the fabrics, it is clear both quilts were made of nineteenth-century fabrics. The "New York Beauty" example has the X layout with spiky borders. Its original solid green fabric has faded to beige. The Turkey red dyed fabric is still bright (see page 64).

The pattern was drafted and printed in house with a copyright date of 1930. Comparing the final pattern to the original quilt, it appears that the person who drafted the pattern followed the antique quilt exactly, even copying the cut-off points and some "fudging" at the intersections. Why he named it "New York Beauty" was not clearly stated in his correspondence.

Another mid-twentieth-century example of the pattern came out soon after the Mountain Mist version. Called "Springtime in the Rockies," the pattern was introduced in the March 21, 1931 issue of *Capper's Weekly.* The format, unlike the New York Beauty, is the right-angled boxed grid. It does not have pieced stars at the intersections or at the corners, but it keeps the spiky borders and the arched units made of small pieces of print fabrics. With the modern bold colors of the 1930s, the pattern is still a stunner (see page 65).

New York Beauty, circa 1865–1870. This red-white-and-blue quilt has an interesting Civil War story. According to the owner, Jeanne Webb, her great-grandmother and grandmother sheltered and nursed a Union soldier following the skirmish at Hoover's Gap in Bedford County, Tennessee. After the war, when the soldier returned home to New York, a family member made this quilt as a token of appreciation. If the story is true, the quilt is a rare example of a "New York Beauty" made in New York. Of course, it would not have been called that in 1865. *From the collection of the Tennessee State Museum.*

Crown of Thorns, circa 1840, 74" x 87". This quilt was made by Mrs. D. P. Walker of Sweetwater Valley, Tennessee. The intricate quilting and fine piecing of this quilt made in the on point layout is a tour de force of the pattern which the family called Crown of Thorns. *From the collection of Carolyn Hodge.*

Detail of Crown of Thorns

Detail of New York quilt

New York Beauty, circa 1890–1910. Sarah Ann Carpenter Simmons, Luverne, Alabama. This quilt made by an African American woman in Alabama uses a variety of fabrics to create a folk-art rendition of the popular pattern. She also used a coral background instead of the traditional white. The quilt shows how the pattern allows for personal creativity and innovation. *From the collection of the Henry Ford Museum (2007.62.1).*

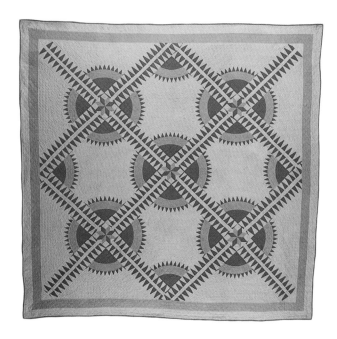

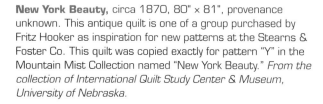

New York Beauty, circa 1870, 80" × 81", provenance unknown. This antique quilt is one of a group purchased by Fritz Hooker as inspiration for new patterns at the Stearns & Foster Co. This quilt was copied exactly for pattern "Y" in the Mountain Mist Collection named "New York Beauty." *From the collection of International Quilt Study Center & Museum, University of Nebraska.*

New York Beauty, 1932, 79" × 79". This quilt is an exact copy of the Mountain Mist pattern "New York Beauty." Rose Tekippe of Fort Atkinson, Iowa, pieced the quilt and her friends, the Twelve Faithful Quilters, quilted it. In the 1933 Sears National Quilt Contest, this quilt reached the final round of just thirty quilts having won third place in the Minneapolis regional round. Over 24,000 quilts were entered in this contest sponsored by Sears, Roebuck & Co. This kind of national attention probably boosted the pattern's popularity and ensured the acceptance of the name "New York Beauty." *Collection of Ada Tekippe Schlick.*

Crown of Thorns also known as Rocky Mountain, 1933, 78" × 79". Lelia Rawls Porter of Hollins, Alabama, also entered this quilt in the 1933 Sears National Quilt Contest. She did not use the newly published Mountain Mist pattern; instead, she may have copied this quilt from an antique quilt in her family. Lelia bought special fabric enough to complete the project. As the contest deadline approached, she was ill, but friends came to the house to finish the quilting. Lelia was happy for the help but worried about the inconsistency of the stitches. The quilt won a green merit award ribbon, but no cash prize. *From the collection of the Birmingham Museum of Art.*

Detail of Sullivan County quilt

Rocky Mountain Road, circa 1920, 69" × 86". This version with an appliqué vine, leaf, and bud instead of the pieced sawtooth units was known as Rocky Mountain Road. Examples from the nineteenth century were documented, but this particular quilt has a bias separate binding which was not available in the 1800s. Pencil markings used to draw on the quilting are still visible. Created in Sullivan County, Tennessee, maker unknown. *From the collection of the Johnson City, Tennessee Mall.*

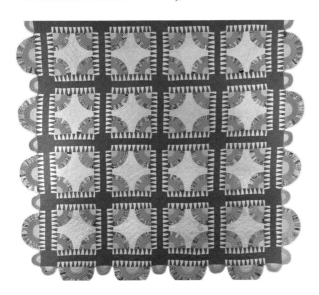

Detail of Meigs County quilt

Springtime in the Rockies, circa 1935, 80" × 86". Though not as well known as the Mountain Mist 1930s version of New York Beauty, this pattern was published in the March 1931 issue of *Capper's Weekly.* The designer chose the squared version, but did not add the stars at the cross points. The deeply scalloped edges made of the same pieced quarter arcs was part of the original pattern design. Made by Sara Moore, Meigs County, Tennessee. *From the collection of Clara Carmichael.*

8

Double Wedding Ring
Sherry Burkhalter

The Double Wedding Ring quilt has been described by some to be the most recognized American quilt. It has long been associated with romance and diamond rings, and has been made with love for many a bride and groom. It is a wonderful way to use buckets full of tiny scrap pieces, yet requires skill to do the curved piecing with precision. Many farm papers, magazines, catalogues, and newspapers throughout the South published patterns for the Double Wedding Ring in the late 1920s and early 1930s. These had similar shapes of interlocking circles with pieced arcs and triangular shaped intersections.

The group of quilts gathered here are examples of the Wedding Ring that were created prior to the 1928 publication that changed the shape of the traditional pattern. These quilts are made with different colors and fabrics than those of the 1920s and '30s, and are more of a squeezed square than interlocking circles. The interlocking arcs come together with a four patch rather than triangular shapes. Many are quite bold and graphic in their color design, and use the fabrics of the 1880s to 1920s. Quilters in the late 1800s frequently used double or triple lines to quilt, sometimes in an all-over arc pattern called Baptist Fan, a common Southern style.

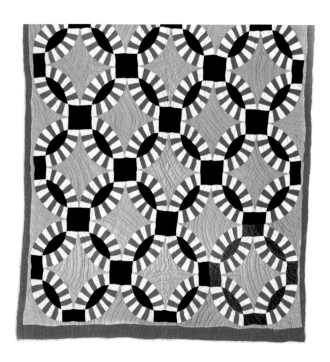

Wedding Ring Quilt, circa 1890, 65" x 76". Quilt maker Lola Demetia Sweeten made this quilt after she moved to Cleveland, Liberty County, Texas in 1896. Owned by Edna Sweeten, wife of Lola's grandson. This graphic artwork is quilted with a double row of a popular Southern arc sometimes called the Baptist Fan. The quilter would use the arc made by her arm moving across the quilt pivoting from the elbow as her pattern. Published in *Lone Stars: A Legacy of Texas Quilts, 1836–1936* by Karoline Patterson Bresenhan and Nancy O'Bryant Puentes, Copyright 1986. *Courtesy of the University of Texas Press.*

Indigo Double Wedding Ring, circa 1900, 79" × 80". The squeezed squares in this quilt are fun to notice as they are a little inconsistent in their size and curve, and are wonderfully scrappy in the random size of the pieces used to make the arcs. The indigo background makes a sharp contrast to the rings. Greensboro, Georgia, maker unknown. *From the collection of Mary Kerr.*

Detail of Indigo Double Wedding Ring quilt

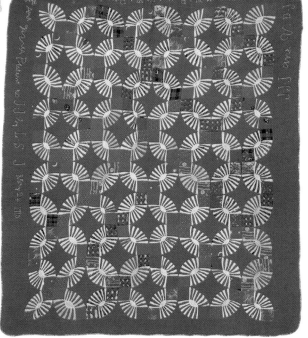

Diamond Ring, circa 1910, 72" × 80". Laura Savannah Stroud Jordan (1876–1952), Jackson County, Georgia. Hand-pieced and hand-quilted cotton. Collection of Vernard Debue Jordan. Georgia Quilt Project #2464. Photo by William C. L. Weinraub, for the Georgia Quilt Documentation Project, Inc. "Around three of the borders is embroidered 'J.J.J. and V.D.J. Age 9 months old when this quilt was finished. He was born August 21, 1909. This quilt was made and given a present to J.J. by L.S.J. May 24, 1910.' Vernard Jordan confirmed that the quilt was a joint gift to John Jackson Jordan and Vernard Debue Jordan, Laura's husband and son, respectively. John Jackson Jordan was born enslaved in 1862 in Jackson County and was freed when he was three years old." As published in *Georgia Quilts: Piecing Together A History*, pg.169.

Wedding Ring, circa 1890, 70" × 81". This quilt is from the Knight Family, from Spio, near Texasville, in Barbour County, Alabama. Note the four-patch piecing is repeated in the large centers of the blocks as well as the intersections of the arcs. There is an interesting diamond border on each side of the quilt, and there are different numbers of blocks on each side, which makes one corner a little skewed. The blocks were made to fit to the border which took some ingenuity. Purchased from Emma Lou Tew, a Knight family member. *From the collection of Sherry Berkhalter.*

Wedding Ring Quilt, circa 1890, 73" × 82". This quilt was made in Ozark, Alabama (Dale County), maker unknown. This quilt is unique in the fact that it uses stars to replace the four-patch intersecting squares. The batting is thick cotton and it shows off the quilting of the Baptist Fan pattern. Photograph by Laura Stakelum at the Waddell House at Landmark Park, Dothan, Alabama. *From the collection of Patricia J. Helton.*

Detail of the Dale County quilt showing a star made with deteriorating brown that was hand-dyed using walnut shells. You can find the vivid reds, shirtings, and checks in the fabrics shown. *Photo by Jana Jones.*

Wedding Ring Quilt, circa 1920, 60" × 78". Headland, Alabama (Henry County). The randomly spaced red is a vivid and heavy woven fabric that sets off the quilt splendidly. The twenty-inch blocks are quilted in large stitches using heavy white thread that adds charm to the red pieces. *Photographed by Laura Stakelum, at Landmark Park, Dothan, Alabama. Family quilt from the Anne Davis collection.*

Wedding Ring Quilt, circa 1900, 79" × 82". This is a graphic quilt that shows well with red as the background. It was made by Anna Liza Johns in Dothan, Alabama. *Photographed on site by Laura Stakelum. From the Landmark Park Quilt Collection in Dothan, Alabama. Donated by D.G. Herring.*

Wedding Ring Quilt, circa 1895, 66" × 71", provenance unknown. Notice the shirtings, mourning prints, and fugitive greens used to create this quilt. *Photographed under the tool shed at Landmark Park, Dothan, Alabama by Laura Stakelum. From the Landmark Park Quilt Collection, donated by John and Retha Dossett.*

Farmer's Fancy, circa 1870, 75" × 93". Frances Andes Harman created this quilt in Mount Clinton, Virginia. The maker passed this quilt to her daughter-in-law, Lydia Harman, who then passed it through three more generations. Two rings of triangles encircle the center plate of twelve blades. An elegant red and green swag border surround the twenty blocks. Quilting is in a diamond grid. *From the collection of the Virginia Quilt Museum (2011.004.001), gift of Frances Brunk Miller, great-great granddaughter of maker.*

9

Farmer's Fancy
Bunnie Jordan

Quilters in the Shenandoah Valley of Virginia produced quilts in a distinctive style that historians now associate with this geographical area. The Farmer's Fancy or Farmer's Delight is a circular pattern similar to the more familiar sunburst and compass blocks. The center of each circle features 8 or 12 petals that could be described as a flower, a star, or a Dresden Plate. Usually these pieced elements alternate in color or value and are encircled by one, two, or three rings of triangles.

The earliest documented Farmer's Fancy quilt block is found on the Suman quilt dated 1846 in the collection of the DAR (Daughters of the American Revolution) (see page 73). Another example, dated 1852, is also in a sampler quilt made by the Ladies of Emmaus Church, New Kent County, Virginia. It is in the collection of the Valentine, Richmond History Center and pictured in the 2006 book *Quilts of Virginia 1607–1899* by the Virginia Consortium of Quilters' Documentation Project. No quilt pattern source from the 1800s has been found, though in the 1850s, *Godey's Lady's Book* published crochet patterns of a similar design. Confirming the adage that there is nothing new, a pattern with only one surrounding ring of triangles can be found in ancient Roman mosaic floor tiles. By the 1890s, the block with one ring of triangles was called Pyrotechnics in Ladies Art Company publications and was also identified as Wheel in *Farm Journal* patterns from 1937 to 1939.

State documentation projects in West Virginia and Virginia found numerous examples of Farmer's Fancy quilts throughout the Shenandoah Valley of Virginia and neighboring areas of West Virginia. This is a beautiful and historic region stretching 200 miles from Harpers Ferry, West Virginia, to Roanoke, Virginia, bordered by the Blue Ridge Mountains

Rocky Road to Kansas, circa 1870, 75" × 75", provenance unknown. Two rings of triangles surround a plate of twelve blades set with a strong cheddar color. The quilting includes double lines in the circles and straight lines on the sashing and borders. *From the collection of Dixie Kaufman.*

Farmer's Fancy, circa 1880, 75" × 93". This quilt was created by Susie Virginia Cline Strickler (1839–1881). She chose bright colors of blue and green for the background and a colorful pieced diamond border. She further challenged tradition with machine quilting. *From the collection of the Virginia Quilt Museum (2014.003.006).*

to the east and the Alleghenies to the west. As early as the 1730s, German and Scots-Irish immigrants began settling here, attracted by religious freedom and the fertile land for farming. Even today it remains an agricultural area and the name Farmer's Fancy or Farmer's Delight seems natural for this farming community.

German Mennonites were lured to the Valley from Pennsylvania and the English and Scots-Irish from eastern Virginia and Maryland. Each of these groups brought their own unique design aesthetic and quilt heritage. Over time these immigrant communities mixed with their neighbors, so designs and patterns were shared and blended.

In *West Virginia Quilts and Quiltmakers* (2000, Ohio University Press), Fawn Valentine reported a characteristic color scheme of green and brown for the wedges of the star in the center of each block. This was found on over half of

the Farmer's Fancy/Farmer's Delight examples documented in West Virginia. All of those were found near the Virginia border and were thought to have originated in the Shenandoah Valley of Virginia. There is no predominant color combination found in the Virginia samples, but the colors red and cheddar yellow appear often. The background color is usually neutral but exuberant examples of blue, cheddar, and green have been found.

Quilting designs are as varied as the triangle scraps that comprise the quilts. Usually of fine stitching, the quilting may be in simple cross-hatch and tiny clamshell, or fancy feathers and symbols such as butterflies and eating utensils. The majority of Farmer's Fancy quilts identified date from the second half of the nineteenth century and are found in this specific geographic area of the South.

Suman Album Quilt, dated 1846 (1843–1847), 110" × 112". This album quilt was made for Lutheran minister John J. Suman and his wife Agnes between 1843 and 1847. Several of its thirty blocks are dated and inscribed by members of congregations in Suman's circuit, which included Jefferson, Berkeley, and Clarke Counties in Virginia. The Farmer's Fancy block of turkey red and green calico prints is inscribed "Mary E. Nicely, March 1846" and includes a verse from Psalm 144. Mary E. Nicely (1825–1908) lived in Middleway, Jefferson County, at the northern end of the Shenandoah Valley. Many of the other blocks are in patterns seen in Baltimore- and Pennsylvania-style album quilts. Nicely's block is the earliest known (so far) of a Farmer's Fancy, which became a favorite up and down the Valley. *From the collection of the DAR Museum (82.130).*

Farmer's Fancy, circa 1845, 91" × 102". An unknown quilt maker created this elegant version. The center fabrics vary, but a single circle of red triangles show consistency, as does the swag border. Quilting includes feathered wreath in the setting squares and one-half inch grid. The five-inch fringe may have been added later. *From the collection of the City of Petersburg Museums (81.10).*

Farmer's Fancy design in crochet work, circa 1850

Farmer's Fancy Barn Quilt. Monroe County, West Virginia, Quilt Trail. *Photo courtesy of Ba Rea.*

Farmer's Fancy, circa 1920, 78" × 81". An unknown quilter from Logan, West Virginia, created her quilt with multicolored scraps of fabric in three rings of triangles surrounding an eight-point red star. Triple red and white sashing separates nine 20" square blocks. *From the collection of Fran Kordek.*

Farmer's Fancy, circa 1875, 76" × 93". An unknown quilter created this version with simpler pieced circles at each intersection. *From the Los Angeles County Museum of Art, Gift of the Betty Horton Collection (M.86.134.36).*

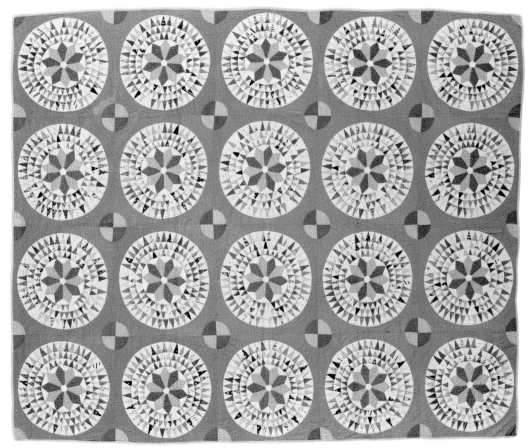

Farmer's Fancy, circa 1880, 76" x 84", quilt maker unknown. This quilt contains Centennial fabric in at least one of the blocks. The quilt has some very interesting quilting, including a fork, knife, spoon, and glass quilted in one area of the textile. The zig-zag border is another feature often associated with the Shenandoah Valley. *From the collection of Taryn Faulkner.*

Farmer's Fancy, circa 1870, 80" × 104". Created by Edith
Shank. *From the collection of Barbara Cline.*

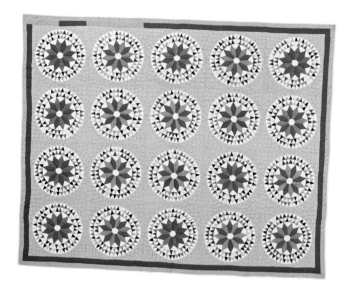

Farmer's Fancy, circa 1880, 72" × 90". Made by Octavia Early Miller. *From the collection of Twilla Risser.*

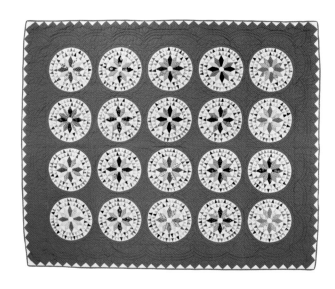

Farmer's Fancy, circa 1930, 86" × 102". This quilt was made by Vera Heatwole and features a single circle of triangles. *From the collection of Margaret Heatwole.*

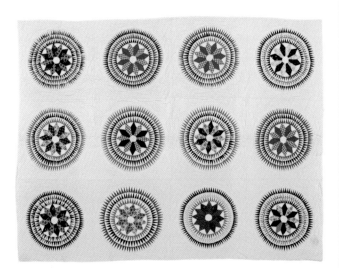

Farmer's Fancy, circa 1880 (quilted in 1930), 61" × 81". This top was created by Dianna Young Richards (1844–1917) in the Shenandoah Valley. One of her descendants, Ida Richards (1886–1966) had it quilted in floral and leaf patterns. *From the collection of the Virginia Quilt Museum (2016.006.001), gift of Samuel Thomas: the Patsy Ann Thomas Collection.*

Farmer's Fancy, circa 1865, 91" × 92". This unknown Shenandoah Valley quilt maker chose a variety of fabrics and included one ring of triangles around a plate of twelve blades. Quilting includes feathers around the circle elements, butterflies, and hearts at the corners. The border is pieced of red triangles. *From the collection of Debbie Cooney.*

Farmer's Fancy, circa 2004, 90" × 107". Barbara Cline redrafted this timeless pattern and paper pieced this version with a scalloped border. *From the collection of Barbara Cline.*

Farmer's Fancy, circa 1890, 76" × 76", provenance unknown. This quilt features a cheddar background with repeated two-color centers and a pieced border. The quilting is concentric rings. *From the collection of Sandra Starley.*

Farmer's Fancy, circa 1875, 76" × 88". This unknown Shenandoah Valley quilt maker repeated two fabrics; the blue and butterscotch prints, for all of the block centers. The surrounding triangles include a variety of colors that complement the center. The quilting includes the double line quilting in clamshell and in the concentric circles. *From the collection of Theresa Grzyb-Wysocki.*

Farmer's Fancy, circa 1890, 76" × 82". This Shenandoah Valley quilt features identical twelve pointed star centers that are surrounded by a double ring of period brown prints with red accents. The background is a poison green print and the backing and binding is a black mourning print. *From the collection of Paula Golden.*

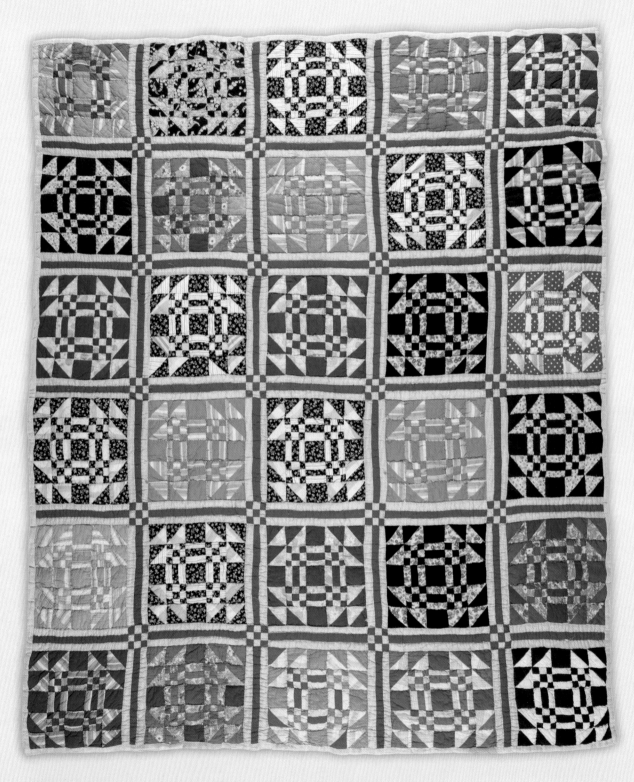

Goose in the Pond, circa 1930–1955, 59" x 71". This quilt was hand pieced and
hand quilted by Leola Heard and Elizabeth Heard Bean of Randolph County, Alabama.
Photo by Steve Goraum. From the collection of Sarah Bliss Wright.

10

The Impact of the Feedsack on Southern Quilts
Sarah Bliss Wright

Cologne Mills (Minnesota) 49 lb. flour sack, manufactured by Bemis Brothers Bag Company. *Photo by Steve Goraum. From the collection of Sarah Bliss Wright.*

Feedsack quilts are lovely reminders of times past when our frugal ancestors either used what they had or they did without. If it couldn't be grown in a garden—flour, sugar, coffee, rice, chicken feed, fertilizer—it was purchased at the nearest general store. Fortunately for quilt lovers, these staple items were packed in cotton bags that, in the hands of resourceful women, not only became clothing and household items for their families, but are preserved in colorful quilts that have survived well beyond their intended purpose. These homemade bed coverings became a genre of textiles now known as "feedsack quilts." The evolution of the feedsack quilt is a story of the resourcefulness of housewives and clever marketing by the nation's bag manufacturers. This trend was especially prevalent in the Deep South.

In the mid 1800s, textile bags replaced wooden barrels as the primary means for transporting and storing household staple items. The first cotton bag fabric was coarse jute or burlap suitable for whole grains and feeds, but finely-milled flour and granulated sugar warranted osnaburg bags that were lighter weight and more tightly woven. These unbleached cotton bags could be imprinted with a customer's logo using permanent dye, a good idea for the mill owner, but a labor-intensive job for the women who wanted to remove the printing and use the fabric. As America entered the twentieth century, that desire to use the "free" fabric in feed, flour, and sugar sacks became a strengthening trend and was embraced by our Southern make-do mentality.

Reuse of bags, often thought to be the result of necessity in the Great Depression, actually began as soon as fabric bags were introduced due to the frugality and practicality

Churn Dash, Monkey Wrench, or Hole in the Barn Door, circa 1930, 60" × 76". This quilt was hand pieced and hand quilted by Leola Heard and Elizabeth Heard Bean of Randolph County, Alabama. *From the collection of Sarah Bliss Wright.*

Scrappy Trip around the World, circa 1930–1955. This quilt was hand pieced and hand quilted by Leola Heard and Elizabeth Heard Bean of Randolph County, Alabama. Leola and Elizabeth apparently did not have enough yellow fabric to complete the border, so they cut a strip of pieced blocks to finish one side . . . . all in the tradition of make-do quilting! *From the collection of Sarah Bliss Wright.*

As hard as the quilt maker may have tried to remove the ink from the sack used on this quilt back, the Bryant's Feed logo is still visible. *Photo by Steve Goraum. From the collection of Sarah Bliss Wright.*

Mosaic Quilt with a flour sack backing, circa 1890, 60" × 82". Greensboro, Georgia, maker unknown. *From the collection of Mary Kerr.*

of rural American women. When the nearest store was miles away, transportation was not easy, and fabric-by-the-yard was limited, women saved and used cotton bag fabric for innumerable household needs from underwear to window curtains. As the nation recovered from the Depression, bag companies realized that simply changing from plain bags to beautiful bags could increase sales by appealing to women who were reusing the fabric. Thus began advertising by bag companies not only to their primary market of grain mills, but to a secondary market as well, the women who repurposed the bags.

Simple gingham bags introduced in the late 1920s ushered in a new textile era, and by the 1930s more than forty bag companies across the nation competed for customers with solid pastels, floral designs, geometrics, and gimmicks. In the 1940s graphic designers produced up-to-date, attractive, and desirable prints, touted by the bag companies as "New York fashions." Women became as particular about the type of sack they wanted as they were about the flour or feed the sack contained.

As dress-print bags gained popularity, bag companies looked for ways to make them easier to reuse: wash-out inks that could be removed with soapy water, paper labels that quickly soaked off, and easy-open chain-stitch closure. A 100 lb. bag yielded more than a yard of dress-print fabric and lots of high-quality thread, manufactured specifically for bag sewing, that was perfect for quilting thread.

The needs of the men and women serving in the armed forces during World War II had an impact on the feedsack industry. Civilians were encouraged to conserve and "make-do" in support of the war. Dressmaking fabric was considered non-essential, but cotton bags, used to transport agricultural products, *were* essential to the war effort. Increased production of dress-print bags put even more beautiful fabrics into American households. As wartime production drew to a close in 1945, secondary use of cotton bags continued to influence the textile industries. Bag companies, in a campaign to "give women what they want!", researched women's preferences and produced bags made from high-quality cotton fabric printed with colorful designs that

Grandmother's Flower Garden, circa 1970, 75" × 90". This quilt was hand pieced by Ruby Green Cagle of Cullowhee, North Carolina. The judicious use of small-print feedsacks and solids yields bursts of bright color in this well designed quilt. *From the collection of the Mountain Heritage Center, Western Carolina University.*

Above & right: **Friendship Star Four-Patch,** circa 1930–1955, 60" × 74". This quilt was hand pieced and hand quilted by Leola Heard and Elizabeth Heard Bean of Randolph County, Alabama. *Photo by Steve Goraum. From the collection of Sarah Bliss Wright.*

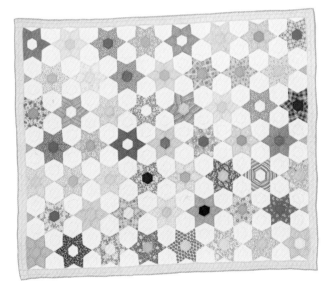

Star, circa 1935, 69" × 81". This scrappy star was created by an unknown quilter from Tuscaloosa, Alabama. *Collection of the Art Fund, Inc., at the Birmingham Museum of Art; gift of Helen and Robert Cargo. Photo by Sean Pathasema.*

vastly increased the possible use of bags for sewing. The farm wife had always relied on feedsack fabrics, but, by mid-century, urban housewives also joined the feedsack recycling trend, making the reuse of cotton bags a way of life in the average American household, from country farms to city apartments.

Throughout the years of double-duty feedsacks, bag companies responded to the demands of the secondary market, women, with dress-prints that reflected the times in which they were produced. Simple gingham and solid colors gave way to plaid, check, stripes, dots, and geometrics. Small prints, large scale floral, *toile,* art deco, and juvenile prints in muted tones and bold colors ensured there was a feedsack for every taste. Eventually, Disney characters such as Donald Duck and Minnie Mouse, movies like *Gone with the Wind* and *Alice in Wonderland*, and television characters like Davy Crockett made their way to feed and flour stores. Such an abundance of diverse fabrics gives feedsack quilts their unique look as the riot of colors and prints give life to every pattern.

By the mid 1950s, the packaging industry was changing. There was a population shift across America. People had

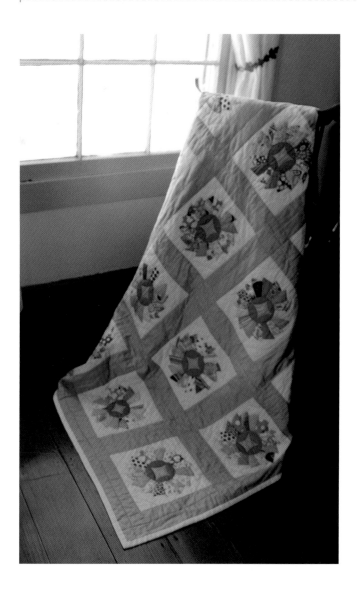

Fan Variation, top circa 1950, quilted in 1960. This top was machine pieced by Mary Catherine Jones Byars of Birmingham, Alabama. This quilt saw little use and gives us an excellent look at flour sack fabrics sold in the city during this era. *From the collection of Sarah Bliss Wright.*

Centennial 100 lb. Egg Mash dress-print feedsack manufactured by Bemis Brothers Bag Company in 1950. *Photo by Steve Goraum. From the collection of Sarah Bliss Wright.*

moved from the farm to the city. Families were smaller and women were working. They didn't buy fifty- and hundred-pound bags of goods any more. They wanted five-, ten-, and twenty-pound bags. Merchants preferred paper bags because they could be made as strong as cotton bags, were easier to stack, and they displayed better on the shelf. Simply put, dress-print bags were single-use bags with an intended reuse that made them cost-effective because they provided free fabric to the housewife. When the housewife didn't buy big quantities of flour and sugar and feed, and affordable fabric was available elsewhere, dress-print bags were no longer in demand.

For more than fifty years, cotton bags had found new purpose in the hands of resourceful women across the nation. The availability and abundance of these printed bags undoubtedly encouraged the making of pieced quilts. Almost every pattern in the quilt inventory has been made, somewhere, sometime, from a stash of dress-print fabric bags and these quilts represent the artistic expression of American women in a distinctive textile era. Feedsack quilts, made from 1930 to 1960 during the height of production of dress-print bags, are now a colorful part of American and Southern quilt history.

Dutch Girl or Sunbonnet Sue, circa 1950, 65" × 77". This quilt was hand appliquéd and hand quilted by Edith Monteith in Dillsboro, North Carolina. The Monteith family owned a mercantile store in Sylva, North Carolina, in the early to mid-twentieth century.

Butterfly, circa 1940, 66" × 80". An unknown maker in Fayette County, Alabama created this unusual variation with tulips. *Collection of the Art Fund, Inc., at the Birmingham Museum of Art; gift of Helen and Robert Cargo. Photo by Sean Pathasema.*

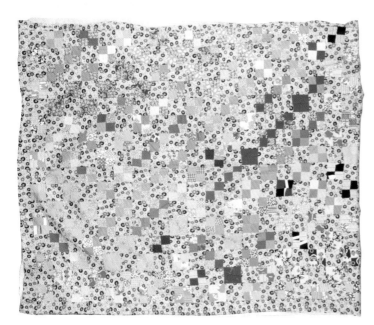

Four Patch, 54" × 67". This quilt was hand pieced by Alice Minerva Enloe Dills in Dillsboro, North Carolina between 1930 and 1949. The quilt maker had enough feedsacks of the same print to create the background and border of this unfinished quilt top. *From the collection of the Mountain Heritage Center, Western Carolina University.*

Country Sampler, circa 1945, 72" × 76". This sampler was made by an unknown quilter in Mississippi. *Collection of the Art Fund, Inc., at the Birmingham Museum of Art; gift of Helen and Robert Cargo. Photo by Sean Pathasema.*

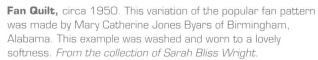

Fan Quilt, circa 1950. This variation of the popular fan pattern was made by Mary Catherine Jones Byars of Birmingham, Alabama. This example was washed and worn to a lovely softness. *From the collection of Sarah Bliss Wright.*

Broken Star, circa 1930, 94" x 94". The solid pink and white provides a calm background for a myriad of patterned diamonds in this fabulous quilt from Tallahassee, Florida. *From the collection of Teddy Pruett.*

Housetop Variation, circa 1930–1955, 63" x 74". This quilt was hand pieced and hand quilted by Leola Heard and Elizabeth Heard Bean of Randolph County, Alabama. The makers made use of scrap quilt blocks to create this bright Housetop variation. Notice parts of a red turtle that was surely a leftover from Turtle Stampede (pages 90–91). *Photo by Steve Goraum. From the collection of Sarah Bliss Wright.*

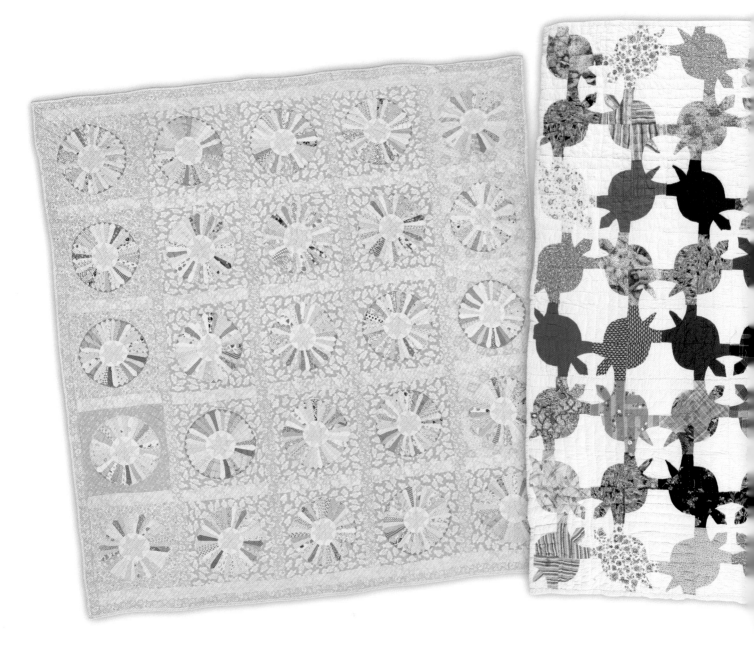

Star in a Sunburst or Circle, circa 1935, 77" × 77". This quilt was made in Tuscaloosa, Alabama, maker unknown. Unusually small strips make up these circles, and a soft color palette gives this lovely quilt its appeal. Patterns such as this one and the popular Dresden Plate were frequently selected to use up small amounts of fabric, yet give a formal look to the quilt. *Collection of the Art Fund, Inc., at the Birmingham Museum of Art; gift of Helen and Robert Cargo. Photo by Sean Pathasema.*

Drunkard's Path–Turtle Stampede, circa 1930–1955, 63" × 74". This quilt was hand pieced and hand quilted by Leola Heard and Elizabeth Heard Bean of Randolph County, Alabama. *Photo by Steve Goraum. From the collection of Sarah Bliss Wright.*

Drunkard's Path Variation, circa 1930–1955, 63" x 74". This quilt was hand pieced and hand quilted by Leola Heard and Elizabeth Heard Bean of Randolph County, Alabama. *Photo by Steve Goraum. From the collection of Sarah Bliss Wright.*

11

Pieced Pine Burr
Mary W. Kerr

Southern quilters are known for their love of spikes, tiny pieces, and impossible patterns. These tendencies all come together in the pieced versions of Pine Burr. While not as plentiful as some of our other pieced blocks, the variations of this pattern showcase the wide range of interpretations we can find throughout the South. The majority of these quilts were found in the Shenandoah Valley, extending southward through the Tennessee Mountains, North Carolina, and Eastern Kentucky.

The earliest versions are from the 1870s and fall into two distinct styles. The first has the pieced units touching so the stars create a secondary circular design between the blocks. The second variation has individual units separated with sashing and cornerstones. Generally, these quilts are completed without a border or finished with simple straight borders.

During the quilt revival of the 1920s and '30s, many traditional patterns were renamed for publication. This pattern came to be called multiple names, including Pine Cones (Nancy Cabot), Philippines (Ladies Art Company #404), Pineapple Cactus (*Kansas City Star* 1932), The Philadelphia Patch (LAC #492), and Pine Burr (Nancy Page and Clara Stone). One can only speculate what they were called by their actual makers.

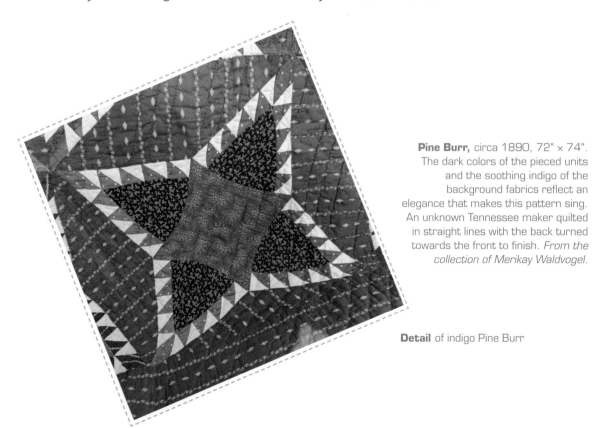

Pine Burr, circa 1890, 72" x 74". The dark colors of the pieced units and the soothing indigo of the background fabrics reflect an elegance that makes this pattern sing. An unknown Tennessee maker quilted in straight lines with the back turned towards the front to finish. *From the collection of Merikay Waldvogel.*

Detail of indigo Pine Burr

Pine Burr, circa 1880, 78" × 92". This thick version from Knoxville, Tennessee is unusual with its pieced sashing and cornerstones. The unknown maker has quilted this with a Baptist Fan design. Note the fading of the purple solids over time . . . the quilt was originally the purple you see at the bottom half of the quilt. *From the collection of Merikay Waldvogel.*

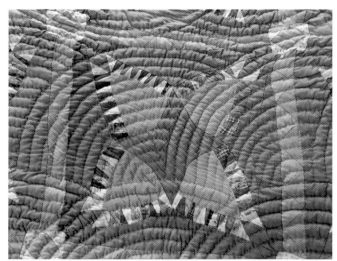

Details of Knoxville Pine Burr

Pine Burr, circa 1880, 68" × 84". This red and green variation features tiny piecing and stars that intersect to create multiple secondary designs. Central Tennessee, maker unknown. *From the collection of Merikay Waldvogel.*

Pine Burr, circa 1900, 72" × 72". This unknown North Carolina quilter set her patriotic blocks with straight sashing and red cornerstones. *From a private collection.*

Pine Burr, circa 1885, 75" × 89". This quilt was made by a member of the Huffman family in Page County, Virginia. This variation has fewer spikes that most and many of the points appear to be intentionally blunted. *From the collection of Karen Alexander.*

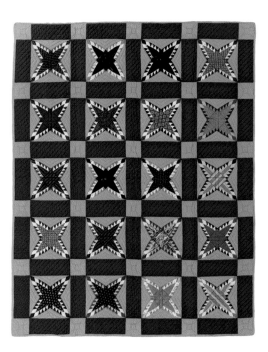

Pine Burr, circa 1870, 66" × 82". This quilt was made by Kentucky quilter, MJ Bowman. She chose the rich color palate of cheddar, teal, and oxblood. *From the collection of the International Quilt Study Center and Museum, University of Nebraska–Lincoln (2014.049.0024).*

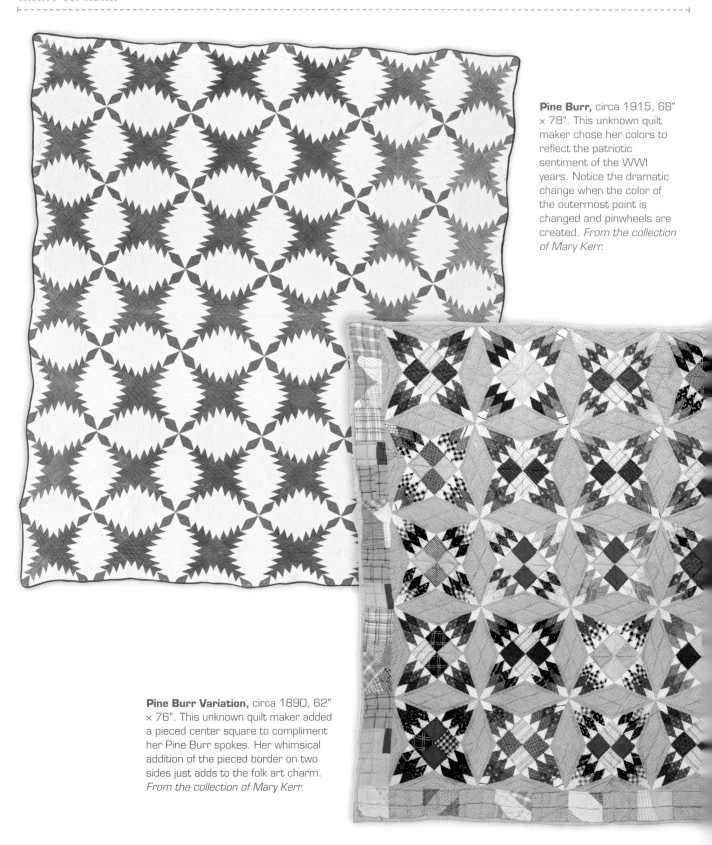

Pine Burr, circa 1915, 68" x 78". This unknown quilt maker chose her colors to reflect the patriotic sentiment of the WWI years. Notice the dramatic change when the color of the outermost point is changed and pinwheels are created. *From the collection of Mary Kerr.*

Pine Burr Variation, circa 1890, 62" x 76". This unknown quilt maker added a pieced center square to compliment her Pine Burr spokes. Her whimsical addition of the pieced border on two sides just adds to the folk art charm. *From the collection of Mary Kerr.*

Pine Burr, circa 1900, 72" x 72". This well loved version was found in Asheboro, North Carolina. The block is simpler than earlier variations and eventually was renamed Rockingham's Beauty (LAC 3203) and Buckeye Beauty (Nancy Cabot 1933). *From the collection of Bonnie Hunter.*

Detail of Asheboro Pine Burr

Rattlesnake Quilt, circa 1925. This quilt was make in Paris, Texas by Willie Yeager. *From the collection of Marcia Kaylakie.*

12

Rattlesnake Quilts
Marcia Kaylakie

Detail of Rattlesnake Quilt, circa 1940, showing heads and tails complete with embroidered eyes and tongues. This quilt was found in a sofa bed at a yard sale in Indiana, but colors clearly indicate a Southern quilt palette. *From the collection of Marcia Kaylakie.*

Pioneers and settlers in the southern and western lands often battled with many natural disasters and along with that, many hostile "critters." Among the worst: the diamondback rattlesnake. Quilters immortalized this threat in a pattern called Rattlesnake, Coiled Rattlesnake, or Diamondback Rattlesnake. Closely resembling a Mohawk Trail or Baby Bunting in pattern, the Rattlesnake pattern can be seen from Virginia west to Texas and Oklahoma, with quilts of this pattern also found in Tennessee, West Virginia, and Georgia. There is some evidence to support the idea that this pattern traveled with one particular family and its members as they migrated south and west across the United States. The quilt pattern appears to have four distinct variations present.

Rattlesnake quilts have their origins in circular patterns and often became adapted into snake variations. Some of the circular patterns include Baby Bunting, Mohawk Trail, Drunkard's Path with Sawtooth, and Fool's Puzzle.

This Rattlesnake variation gives the illusion of a coiled snake. One of the examples actually has additional heads and tails as well as embroidered eyes and tongues.

Another popular variation occurs when curved piecing creates the curves of the snake. These fan or arc pieces are arranged to replicate the movement of a snake across the quilt.

Some Rattlesnake quilts are one of a kind patterns and are created individually with no known pattern.

Snake Trail top, circa 1930, 72" × 92". This unknown quilt maker chose bright prints and red fans to create this snake variation with a pieced border. *From the collection of Mary Kerr.*

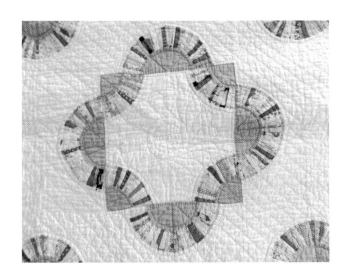

Detail of Oklahoma Snake Ring

Oklahoma Snake Ring, circa 1930, 76" × 92". A family near Texarkana, Arkansas named this Baby Bunting Variation, Oklahoma Snake Ring. It contains over 6,000 pieces. *From the collection of Polly Mello.*

Baby Bunting, circa 1915, 68" x 85". Provenance unknown.

Rattlesnake Quilt, circa 1930, provenance unknown. *From the collection of Polly Mello.*

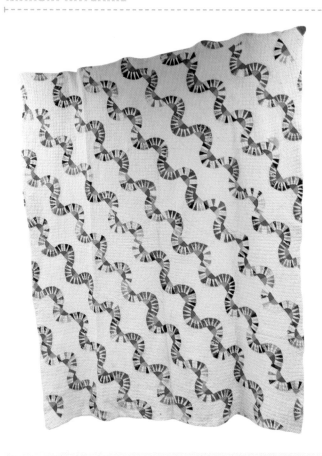

Detail of Snake's Trail

Snake's Trail, circa 1890. This Fort Worth, Texas quilter pieced the center fans of her snake trail. The arcs are constructed with a wide variety of period prints set on shirtings. *From the collection of Polly Mello.*

Rattlesnake block fragment, circa 1890. *From the collection of Polly Mello.*

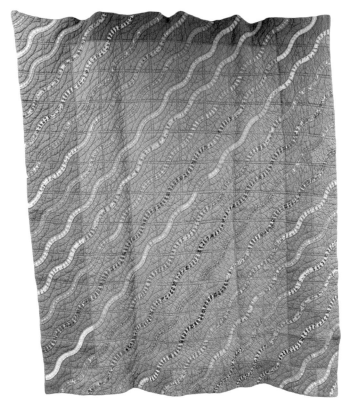

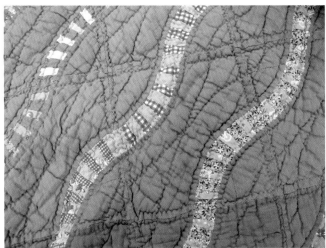

Detail of Snake's Trail

Snake's Trail, circa 1930, 68" × 82". Small scale snakes slither through the green grass. Provenance unknown. *From the collection of Polly Mello.*

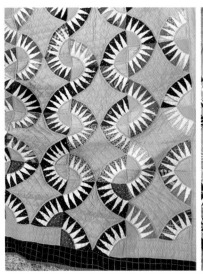

Snake's Trail, circa 1940, 68" × 84". This version was created in Milton, Florida, maker unknown. *From the collection of Alma Moates.*

Rattlesnake, circa 1890, provenance unknown. *From the collection of Clyde and Judy Metzger.*

13

Seven Sisters
Sandra Starley

The Seven Stars or Seven Sisters quilt pattern has a rich and intriguing history. With imagery spanning centuries from starry night skies full of mythical Greek goddesses, tales of Confederate star flags and lovely sisters from Old Virginia, and finally to the simply descriptive, since the block is composed of seven stars, there is a lot of mystery and conjecture about the pattern's origins and what the different names really mean.

The Mississippi Quilt Project documented a "fondness for the star pattern known as 'Seven Sisters,' a name taken from the cluster of stars in the constellation of Taurus with the astronomical name of 'the Pleiades.' Some oldtimers thought you could predict the weather according to the number of 'sisters' you could see on any given night, and that may have contributed to its popularity among Mississippi quilters." The Greek myth of the seven daughters of the Titan God Atlas, trapped in the heavens, has been around for thousands of years. It features seven sisters who have become stars and thus applies equally to both main block names.

A very Southern origin for the Seven Stars name is related to the beginning of the Civil War and the seven stars on the first Confederate flag. These stars represented the

"Seven Stars is a romantic sounding name, but the quilt really deserves this lofty title. It's a beauty."

—Ruby McKim, *101 Patchwork Patterns*, 1931

Seven Sisters, circa 1900, 74" × 82". An unknown Tennessee quilt maker has set her star blocks with cheddar. This is an uncommon choice for Seven Sisters but oh those fabrics shine! *From the collection of Teddy Pruett.*

Detail of Seven Sisters

Detail of Seven Sisters quilt from Spiro, Kentucky

Seven Sisters, 72" × 80". This quilt top was pieced in 1934 by Vira Alice Brown (one of seven sisters) from Spiro, Kentucky. The top was hand quilted in 1999 by her niece, Carol Ann Noe White. *From the collection of Carol Ann Noe White.*

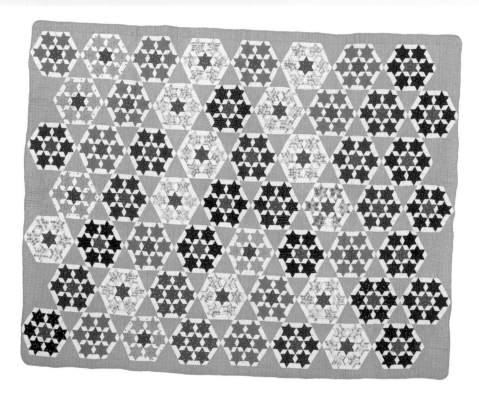

Seven Sisters, circa 1900, 64" × 86". East Tennessee, maker unknown. *From collection of Sharon Waddell.*

Seven Sisters, circa 1900, 72" × 84". This badly damaged variation was rescued in Greensboro, Georgia. Maker unknown. *From the collection of Mary Kerr.*

first seven states to secede from the Union. In addition to the seven star flags, there were other seven star textiles made at the time and so it is possible that some people selected the pattern to reflect their political positions, or to "vote with their needles." While the seven star flag was used for less than three months in 1861, the powerful symbolism of such a significant flag likely inspired some quilters to recreate it through this pattern.

Nancy Cabot's 1933 pattern for Seven Sisters contains another alleged Southern origin story: "The pride of Virginia were the seven lovely daughters of the Fowler family. They were known everywhere in the state. To these famous sisters has been dedicated today's quilt pattern—'Seven Sisters.' Other names for the same design are 'Seven Stars' and 'Virginia Pride.'" Written in a time when romanticism reigned over historical accuracy, this attribution appears to be pure fiction. No other sources use the Virginia Pride name or reference the lovely Fowler sisters, including Fowler family histories.

While Seven Sisters is the most recognized name today, the pattern was originally published as Seven Stars in the 1895 Ladies Art Company catalog. The descriptive Seven Stars in a Cluster, *Capper's Weekly*, 1928, followed as well as Seven Stars, *Kansas City Star*, 1931. In 1933, the Seven Sisters name appeared in Nancy Cabot's column. Other names include Boutonniere (*Kansas City Star*, 1931); Building Blocks (Nancy Cabot, 1933); Star Bouquet (*Home Art Studios, World Herald*, 1933); and Rolling Star (*Kansas City Star*, 1936). In 1933, Mrs. Evans, a contributor to Nancy Page's column, reported on a quilt she received from her Arkansan grandmother which the "grandmother called 'Seven Stars' but Mrs. Evans (wanted) to rechristen it and call it 'Seven Great Lights.'" That name did not go any further.

Seven Stars/Sisters is an intricate and visually engaging block composed of seven stars grouped in a staggered set to create a hexagon or a circle design. The pattern is generally made with seven diamond stars pieced into a hexagon shape with diamonds or hexagons between the stars. The rarer group has seven diamond stars or sometimes flower shapes that are pieced into circles and then usually set into square blocks. With myriad ways to construct the blocks, to set them, and then to color them, "Seven Stars" may really refer to the infinite number of versions one can create of this versatile block. The hexagon pattern is not exclusively Southern but it is especially popular in the South and most often made there. The Circle of Stars blocks seem to be wholly of Southern origin.

It is a challenging pattern. McKim (see chapter epigraph) understated that point: "Of course this is a rather difficult one to piece, as blocks sew in, rather than all going in straight seams." Hexagon versions tend to be hand pieced often with the use of the English paper piecing technique which employs diamond shaped paper templates. Each star section is created with six diamonds. Some are even pieced as seven small hexagonal stars that are joined to create a larger hexagon star (A Little Girl's Star, *Kansas City Star*, 1950). Hexagon blocks are usually stagger set to create an allover design. Mary Elizabeth Johnson noted in *Star Quilts* that if white is used for the ground in the stars and between them, "the stars appear to twinkle in circular clusters. An interesting secondary pattern resembling a six-pointed snow crystal is formed in the white areas." If a color is used for the outer triangles (between the hexagons) a secondary design of large shared six-pointed stars is formed.

The circular versions like the hexagons are almost always hand pieced but the individual stars have more variety than seen in the hexagon versions. The stars may be pieced in delicate six sectioned flower shapes or hand appliquéd in single large star shapes. The circular versions frequently have an additional design element of an outer ring of sawteeth or diamonds framing the stars. They are also more often set in sashed blocks. Curiously, all of the vintage published patterns and pattern reference books show hexagon blocks rather than any of the circular patterns; yet we frequently find Southern quilts made using these circular pattern variations.

Seven Sisters, 1918, 68" × 82". This quilt was made by Cella Jane Harris Patton (1896–1929) in Vortex, Kentucky. She married Grover Patton in March of 1918 and created this quilt with scraps of her wedding dress. After she died during the birth of her fifth child, Grover married her older sister Emma Harris Patton. Together they raised a blended family of seven children. From the collection of Cella's granddaughter, Cindy Rennells.

Detail of Patton quilt

The back of Patton quilt. Note the feedsack backing and the Baptist fan quilting.

Star Ring top, circa 1900, 70" x 84". This Ring of Stars variation is not technically a Seven Sisters pattern as there are only six stars. There are numerous variations on this pattern and opportunities to play. The white fabric in this top are recycled feedsacks. *From the collection of Mary Kerr.*

Seven Sisters Doll Quilt, circa 1900, 14"
x 14", provenance unknown. *From the
collection of Karen Alexander.*

Seven Sisters, circa 1840, 94" × 96". This unique variation features delicate stars and a chintz border. It has been hand pieced and hand appliquéd, quilted by hand in one-half-inch rows. Provenance unknown. *From the collection of Neva Hart.*

Detail of Hart quilt

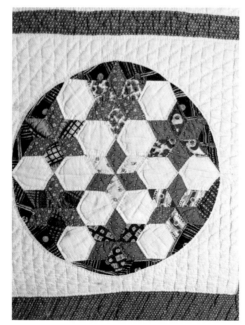

Detail of Spence quilt

Star Cluster, circa 1860, 80" × 100". This Seven Sisters variation features circular units that have been set with sashing. Provenance unknown. *From the collection of Catherine Spence.*

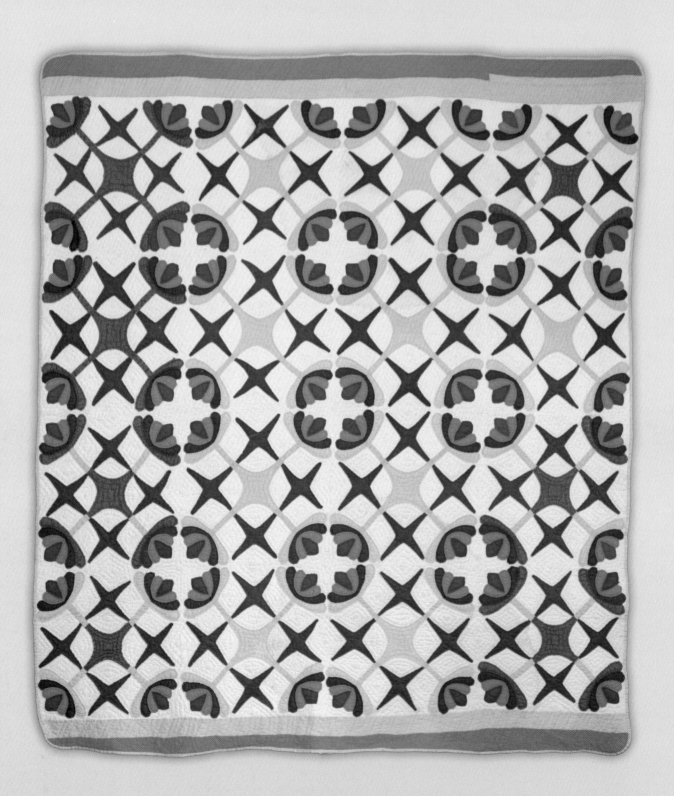

14

Southern Florals
Lisa Erlandson

Quilters have long drawn inspiration from the world around them. Daily life, bible verses, and nature are heavily referenced in quilt block names and motifs. Among the most popular are floral patterns. While quilters in all areas enjoyed flowers, Southern quilters certainly had an abundance of colorful flora to influence their design choices.

The floral patterns found in these quilts are numerous and include both pieced and appliquéd patterns. While most of these patterns may also appear in other regions, there appear to be certain common themes across the south. Variations of both lily and tulip motifs appear to have been favorites over the centuries. There are also patterns representing flowers that are indigenous to the area, especially in twentieth-century quilts. The quilts shown here represent a variety of eras and workmanship but the styles have a common thread. Each of these quilts was made in the South by Southern quilters and they show a certain spirit.

Crossed Coxcomb, circa 1870, 66" × 75". Eastern Tennessee, maker unknown. *From the collection of Cindy's Antique Quilts, Cindy Rennells.*

The size and arrangement of blocks varies a great deal in these quilts. Both fine and primitive workmanship are found. There are quilts that have been put away and treasured as well as those that have been worn from the use that the quilt maker intended. We know the maker and origin of a few of these quilts but like makers elsewhere, few Southern women took the extra time or effort to document their quilts or the reason that the quilt was created.

Nineteenth century floral quilts may show more regional differences than those from the twentieth century. While there was an abundance of fabric in certain areas of the United States, the technology of the times dictated the colors that were available. The color schemes may be those used in quilts made across the country or the quilt could be made with color combinations that were more commonly southern. Many of the floral quilts of the south utilize solid colors at a time when quilts from other areas of the country were using numerous prints. Southern quilt makers would not have had as many choices in fabrics as their New England counterparts.

As the twentieth century dawned, women gained exposure to a larger variety of information through the wide distribution of publications such as newspapers and magazines. They were given the opportunity to choose from a wider selection of patterns. Some of these patterns were offered freely in the publications while others were available to order. It seems logical that women might order a pattern that they were familiar with. It is during this time that we see the graceful appliqués of dogwood and tulips as well as other floral motifs that the quilters could also find in their gardens. These quilts may use fabrics similar to quilts

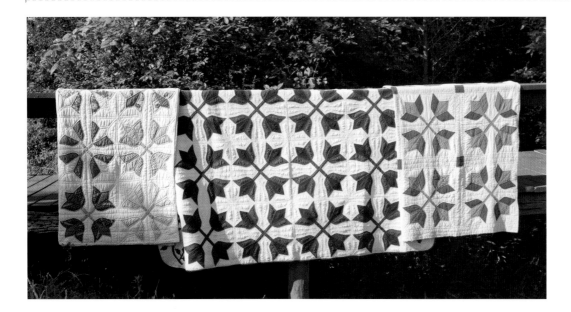

Three Tulip Quilts, *photo by Lisa Erlandson*

Carolina Lily, circa 1870, 80" × 92", unknown provenance. Note the fine workmanship and the pieced sashing. *From the collection of Teddy Pruett.*

Floral Sampler, circa 1860, 92" × 92". This sampler of floral motifs was made by an unknown Georgia quilt maker. *From the collection of Carolyn Miller*

made from coast to coast and the workmanship of Southern quilts is no different than that found in any other region—some quilt makers were exceptional seamstresses with a wonderful quilting stitch and others made quilts that were quickly and crudely constructed.

In any time period, floral designs, by their nature, are more difficult than many other patterns and as a result, we may be seeing the best work of the maker when we look at these quilts. Appliqué is a natural technique when trying to make a representational or realistic pattern and as most quilters will agree, appliqué is better suited to those with more experience in sewing. That is not to disrespect the pieced floral patterns. These patterns demand accuracy to create the realistic look of a peony or a lily.

Are there more floral quilts in the south? Probably not. Are there patterns that are distinctly Southern? Maybe. Have Southern quilters put a Southern spin on floral quilts through use of color and repetition of certain patterns? Absolutely.

Carolina Lily, circa 1900, 72" × 78". North Texas, maker unknown. This version reflects its Southern roots with a thick batting and Baptist Fan quilting. *From the collection of Cindy's Antique Quilts, Cindy Rennells.*

Peony, circa 1870, 87" × 97". Texas, maker unknown. Quilted in the center of this quilt are the initials "EML." *From the collection of Cindy's Antique Quilts, Cindy Rennells.*

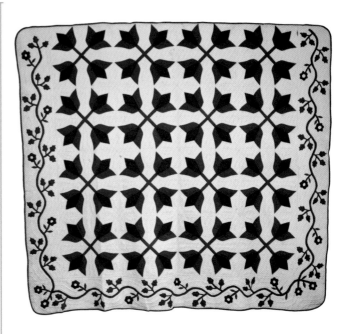

Crossed Tulips, circa 1870, 83" × 91". North Carolina, maker unknown. *From the collection of Cindy's Antique Quilts, Cindy Rennells.*

Tulip, circa 1870, 78" × 94". Virginia, maker unknown. *From the collection of Cindy's Antique Quilts, Cindy Rennells.*

Dogwood, circa 1925, 76" × 94". Provenance unknown. *From the collection of Beverly Birkmire.*

Counter-clockwise from above:
Tulip quilt top, circa 1900, 84" × 92". North Carolina, maker unknown. *From the collection of Lisa Erlandson.*

Coxcomb, circa 1870, 78" × 81". Virginia, maker unknown. *From the collection of Cindy's Antique Quilts, Cindy Rennells.*

Dahlia, circa 1940, 76" × 88". Texas, maker unknown. *From the collection of Lisa Erlandson.*

Tulip Bouquet, circa 1920, 68" × 84". Made by Birdie Mae Hart Wade in Scurry County, Texas. *From the collection of Lisa Erlandson.*

Rose Bouquet, circa 1870, 66" × 86". This quilt was made by Martha "Mattie" Wood Petty in Sherman, Texas. She was born in Carthage, Missouri, in 1851, and came to Texas in the early 1870s. *From the collection of Carolyn Miller.*

Detail of Rose Bouquet

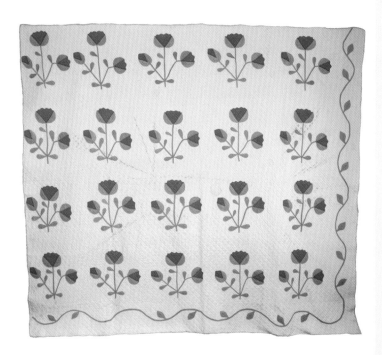

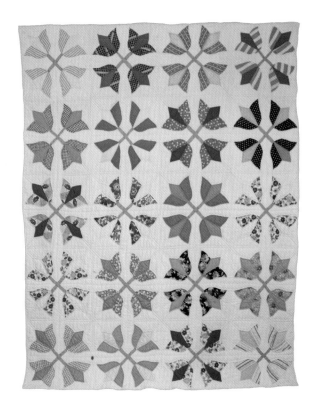

Coxcomb Bouquet, circa 1860, 87" × 97". Southern Kentucky, maker unknown. *From the collection of Cindy's Antique Quilts, Cindy Rennells.*

Crossed Tulips, circa 1940, 64" × 84". Cooke County, Texas, maker unknown. *From the collection of Lisa Erlandson.*

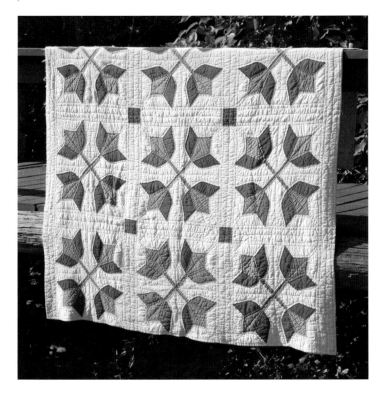

Detail of Florida Crossed Tulips

Crossed Tulips, circa 1930, 66" × 82".
North Florida, maker unknown. *From the
collection of Teddy Pruett.*

Tulip 4-Block, circa 1940, 76" × 79". Provenance
unknown. *From the collection of Mary Kerr.*

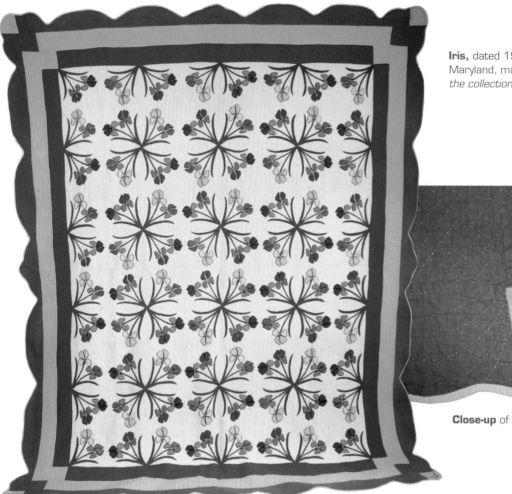

Iris, dated 1944, 82" × 94".
Maryland, maker unknown. *From the collection of Lisa Erlandson.*

Close-up of embroidered corner

Detail of Iris

Ohio Rose, circa 1930, 74" × 92". McCracken County,
Kentucky. *From the collection of Gloria Myrick Meriwether.*

Detail of Ohio Rose

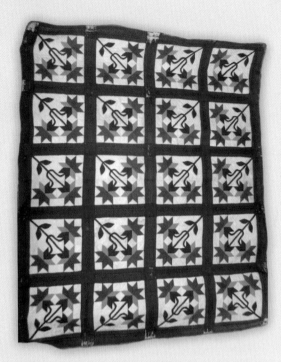

Carolina Lily, circa 1870. South Carolina, maker unknown. *From the collection of Lynn Gorges.*

Washington Feather, circa 1870, 77" × 77". Piedmont, North Carolina, maker unknown. *From the collection of the International Quilt Study Center and Museum, University of Nebraska–Lincoln (2014.049.0003).*

Crown of Thorns, circa 1860, 66" × 88". Guilford County, North Carolina, maker unknown. Note the wonderful appliquéd sashing and the whimsical addition of the zigzag border on one side. *From the collection of the International Quilt Study Center and Museum, University of Nebraska–Lincoln (2014.049.0005).*

Peony Variation, circa 1890, 62" × 80". Randolph County, North Carolina, maker unknown. *From the collection of the International Quilt Study Center and Museum, University of Nebraska–Lincoln (2014.049.0022).*

15

Tricolor Quilts:
How the Germans of Pennsylvania Influenced a Color Palette and Style in the South
Lynn Lancaster Gorges

While viewing antique quilts with other textile historians over the years a common thread seemed to be present. When a quilt made of the color combination blue/green, golden/orange, and oxblood brown, with a white background, would be shown, the group would immediately say that the quilt must have been made in Pennsylvania or the South. Oftentimes it would have been made in North Carolina. This began to intrigue many of us who study quilt history. We wanted to know why this seemed to be regional and why there was possibly a connection to Pennsylvania.

It seemed that my collection of quilts in this color scheme began to grow rather unintentionally. I was drawn like a magnet to "those colors." They were not always identical colors, but they were certainly similar enough for it to register with me as "those colors." Most of the time there would be at least a splash of orange or even a large amount of orange. Then again, at times the quilter would use only the blue/green and the brown. In studying the state quilt documentation books I saw many of these quilts. They even showed up in Texas, Indiana, and West Virginia. Those quilts showed how the colors traveled with the new settlers from Virginia, North Carolina, and South Carolina, or possibly they made their way into those states with relatives who visited.

The teal blue/orange/oxblood quilts are seen first around 1850. The fabrics are usually solid color fabrics, not printed. To our modern day sensibilities these colors seem a bit odd at first. The red and green appliqués seem more historic and appropriate for the 1800s. However upon doing research the use of this color combination resonates through many other art forms during the mid- to late-1800s. It is even seen in tiles that cover the floor of the Capitol in Washington, DC, on the House of Representatives side (page 126).

The Pennsylvania Germans were using this tricolor combination in the glazes of their earthenware pottery made of red (orange) clay. This tradition followed the people who migrated in the 1700s from Pennsylvania via the Great Wagon Road that went from Pennsylvania through the Virginia Shenandoah Valley into the Piedmont area of North Carolina. Ultimately that route took the Moravians to a settlement called Wachovia, now called Old Salem. The Moravians in the Pennsylvania area and in the North Carolina settlement used these colors in their pottery and in their paint selections for their homes and their painted furniture (page 126).

The colors are seen in Frakturs created to commemorate special events in the lives of Mennonites in Pennsylvania and North Carolina. Other people of German heritage utilized these tricolors in the Lexington area of South Carolina.

Is it possible that the glaze recipes used for ceramic earthenware and tiles, and the paint recipes, were made of natural pigments found in the earth of the Piedmont/ hill regions of these locales, and then found themselves repeated in fabric dyes? The first textile mill in the south to begin to dye textiles was in Alamance County, North Carolina, in 1853. Old Salem is close by. They were already at that time making similar pottery in those areas.

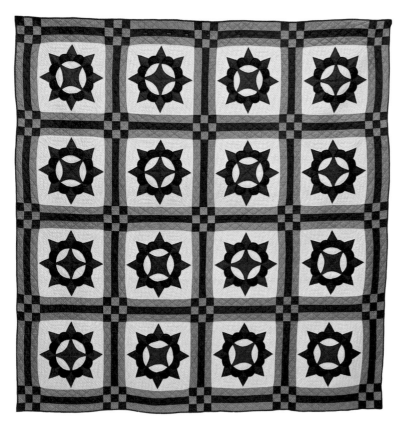

Detail of May quilt

Full Blown Tulip, circa 1860. This quilt was made by Tabitha Bynum May in Farmville, North Carolina. *From the collection of the May Museum in Farmville, North Carolina.*

Rocky Mountain, circa 1870, 83" × 83", provenance unknown. This stunning cheddar and teal combination features a chintz border. *From the collection of Sandra Starley.*

Star Variation, circa 1850, 64" × 82". This quilt was made by an unknown North Carolina quilter. It features four different sizes of pieced stars. *From the collection of Mary Kerr.*

More research needs to be done to determine more about the use of the tricolor combination and the blue/green and brown combination. To those of us who are fascinated by the use of these colors we are just scratching the surface of the dyes used for cotton fabrics and the textile manufacturing growth in the south. Many of the quilts demonstrate the use of unstable dyes during that time period. The brown has often turned to a khaki color probably after a few washings. There are so many factors that contribute to why these colors were often used in these areas.

For now we do know that the women of the last half of the nineteenth century in Pennsylvania and in the states that were part of the Southern migration routes—Indiana, Texas, Georgia, South Carolina, North Carolina, Tennessee, and Kentucky—loved these colors and shared their appliqué style patterns and other patterns. Oh to go back and attend one of the many fairs of those time periods to see the women admiring the use of these "earth tones" that so blended with the new land they were settling.

Pottery display at Museum of Early Southern Decorative Arts (MESDA) in Winston-Salem, North Carolina. *Photo courtesy of Lynn Gorges.*

Tile from the US Capitol Building, circa 1850

Sideboard, circa 1850. *From the collection of the Lexington County Museum, Lexington, South Carolina.*

Whig Rose, circa 1870. South Carolina, maker unknown.
From the collection of Lynn Gorges.

Carolina Lily, circa 1870. South Carolina, maker unknown.
From the collection of Lynn Gorges.

Pomegranate, circa 1880. South Carolina, maker unknown. *From the collection of Lynn Gorges.*

Close-up of Pomegranate block

Coxcomb and Currants, circa 1870, 74" x 75". Provenance unknown. Though only two colors, this example fits the aesthetics of the tricolor quilts found in the region. Note the embroidered details and the typical Southern echo quilting. *From the collection of Mary Kerr. Photography by Phil Warish.*

Detail of Coxcomb and Currants.
Photography by Phil Warish.

Whig's Defeat, circa 1870, 80" × 82". Quinns, Virginia, maker unknown. In 1930 this Whig's Defeat variation was renamed Fanny's Favorite by *Caper's Weekly. From the collection of Sandra Starley.*

Detail of Virginia Whig's Defeat

16

Whig's Defeat
Gaye Rice Ingram

The Whig's Defeat pattern is one of three quilt patterns believed to have arisen in the American South, the others being Seven Sisters [see Chapter 13] and Rocky Mountain Road [see Chapter 7]. The Whig's Defeat pattern is first noted in the mid-South, among the Scots-Irish in North Carolina and Tennessee. Like the other two patterns, its construction demonstrates the early Scots-Irish preference for intricate piecing over appliqué, a preference in this case taken to what seems an absurd extreme. Each unit had 145 pieces. In the early examples every part is pieced, even the

"fingers" that spring from the center part of the block. Its transmission into the Deep South and Texas seems principally the work of Tennessee families and citizens, among them the sprawling Polks of North Carolina and Tennessee.

Quilt historians long have traced the origin of this pattern to the presidential election of 1844 in which the Democrat James K. Polk defeated the Whig Henry Clay. In it, they have seen evidence of women's growing political consciousness. In a 2017 exhibition at the St. Louis Museum of Art, *Textiles: Politics and Patriotism*, curator Zoe A. Perkins claims the rise of quilting in the nineteenth century gave women, "who did not yet possess the right to vote, a tactile way to express their political views." She cites the Whig's Defeat and the Whig Rose as particular evidence of women's use of quilts to express their personal political views.

Yet the pattern was popular at least twenty years earlier than the famous election, and its history strongly suggests later incarnations originated in family domestic traditions, not political passions. In the extant Whig's Defeat quilts may be seen not so much a political pattern as a migration pattern. Southern families were on the move south and west in the period before the Civil War. The Louisiana Purchase, the War of 1812, Indian treaties, and property surveys had opened the rich lands to settlers in present-day Alabama, Mississippi, Louisiana, and Florida. Texas lay on the horizon, already home to a thriving Anglo-American community.

Women first appeared at political rallies in the presidential election of 1840. These affairs attracted huge crowds and had always been notoriously rowdy. Long tables improvised from boards and sawhorses sagged under the

Whig's Defeat quilt top, circa 1880. Provenance unknown. The fabrics used, additional elements, and spacing lead one to believe it may have been made in South Carolina or Georgia. *From the collection of Gaye Rice Ingram. Photography by Kevin Beasley.*

weight of barbecued sides of beef and pork fresh from nearby spits. Kegs of whiskey quenched the thirst of the electorate. Generalized brawls, eye-gouging, and broken bones were commonplace, and the more eloquent the oratory, the more likely the rally was to erupt in generalized violence. So serious had the problem become that in 1840, Whig politicians tried something new: reasoning that in the presence of ladies, men generally behaved in a more civilized manner, they invited women to their rallies. Thrilled at being included in these major social events, Whig ladies sewed banners and flags, prepared their finest recipes, and turned out as for a church picnic. In return, they had the privilege of standing in the crowd with their escorts or sitting in a special section set aside for them and listening to the oratory of candidates and their supporters. So effective was the presence of women in bringing order to Whig rallies, the Democrats followed suit in the election of 1844.

Their letters and diary entries suggest women were pleased to be included in these lively communal gatherings and that what impressed them was the socializing and the oratorical eloquence of the speakers. Historians have found no evidence of women from Democratic families whipping up fine pies to take to a Whig political rally or of Whig wives showing up with a cake at Democratic rallies. That voting was men's duty in the family appears generally unchallenged by women who attended the rallies. They responded in ways consistent with women's roles of the time.

Sometime after the election of 1844, a quilt pattern that sometimes became known as Whig's Defeat appeared, mostly in middle Tennessee and the Sweetwater Valley of Tennessee at first, then in Texas, parts of Louisiana, and eventually all over the South. What seems likely is that a valued quilt in the Polk family, probably one popular in the region, was given a name change after the election. It might well have been the pattern's association with the Polks, the region, or even with the defeated party that the pattern gained symbolic importance in some parts. Whatever its source, it was not a new pattern to Tennesseans in 1844, and Tennessee women seem to have missed the memo about its political message.

The earliest extant example of a quilt in this pattern seems to have been made for the wedding of Margaret Poindexter McCammon to Francis P. Pettitt in December 1824, in Surry County, North Carolina. The Pettitts took it with them when, along with a group of other Scots-Irish family members, they moved to McMinn County, Tennessee, around 1834. Within the family it was known as the Ladyfingers quilt, a name that might have referred to the resemblance of the five feathers in the pattern to a common wildflower. The McCammon quilt is currently in the collection of the Tennessee State Archives.

Quilt historians Bets Ramsey and Barbara Brackman note early quilts made west of the mountains tended to be made of one or two colors and white, perhaps out of a desire to permit fine quilting as well as fine piecing or perhaps because of a lack of variety in materials available. In the McMinn County Museum in Athens, Tennessee, is a fragment of another early example of this pattern in which the maker used what appears to be home-dyed red and green along

with another early version of the same quilt. Each unit had 145 pieces. Michael Luster's 1986 book *Stitches in Time* shows a quilt in this pattern that he dates to 1826 and whose maker called it Lady Fingers.

It is possible quilts in this pattern existed in the Polk and Knox families, who had lived in Mecklenburg County, North Carolina, before they crossed the mountains. We know some family members were already using it and continued to make quilts in the pattern. But no one has located a quilt specifically dedicated to political purposes.

Early association of the pattern with Tennessee can be seen in an elaborate 1850 wedding quilt discussed by Kathlyn Fender Sullivan in *North Carolina Quilts* (1988). Made in the familiar pattern, but with smaller blocks and intricate striping, the wedding quilt of North Carolinian Louisa Green Furches Etchison was named "Tennessee Beauty" (page 138). Its early existence and continued popularity in North Carolina is clear in the collections of John Rice Irwin and Robert Timberlake, who popularized the pattern in the late twentieth century.

Detail of Mobile quilt

Whig's Defeat, circa 1860. Mobile, Alabama, maker unknown. This damaged variation features unique colors and elaborate sashing. *From the collection of Vicki Crooms.*

Whig's Defeat, circa 1840. Surry County, Virginia, maker unknown. The narrow sashing suggests the blocks were made by one person and finished by another. *From the collection of Gaye Rice Ingram.*

Detail of Surry County Whig's Defeat

This old pattern seems to have been known primarily as a wedding quilt. Wedding quilts traditionally were made in the most demanding patterns, and with its acute angles and bias seams sewed to bias seams, this pattern is among the most difficult. It also allows large spaces for fine quilting. The presence of hearts in the quilting, often accompanied by a date and two names is common to the finest examples. More than half the examples I've seen have had hearts as a quilting motif and many include initials and a date in the quilting or embroidery.

The greatest number of remaining nineteenth-century examples of this pattern, made in a time when patterns were passed within family or friendship groups in the rural South, are found in East Tennessee and in Texas or along trails between the two. The critical issue in the election of 1844 was, in fact, Texas. Tennesseans had a long history with Texas and the Texas Republic, and branches of some of the state's most important families were among its first citizens. Walkers, Robertsons, Polks. Knoxes, and their allied families—these and many more leading Tennessee families became leaders in the new territory. So it is not unusual that a quilt pattern familiar to middle Tennessee would also become familiar to Texans.

That this pattern is more associated with families than with politics may be seen in two Louisiana examples.

Leonidas Polk, the first Episcopalian Bishop of Louisiana, and his cousin William Polk, owned plantations south of the Red River in Rapides and Avoyelles Parishes. When their younger relative Lamar Polk's goods were sold in the 1990s, a bold Whig's Defeat quilt of the late nineteenth century was among the items in the estate. The owner of Griffin's Antiques in Bunkie, Louisiana, bought the quilt. Shortly thereafter, Texas quilt collector Carolyn Roller Miller came upon it and researched its history. An earlier and more refined version of the pattern in red, white, and blue colors adorns a Louisiana French colonial bed at Kent House Museum in nearby Alexandria, also linked to the large and widespread family.

Discerning motivation for quilts nearly two centuries after they were made is difficult. After all, most who moved to Texas from Tennessee were probably confirmed Democrats, and it is entirely possible their wives took some pleasure in making a quilt that declared their home a Democratic Tennessee home. But months and years in archives in Georgia, Tennessee, North Carolina, and Alabama have given me no reason to believe politics was the principal motivation. Rather, the pattern itself, the challenge it posed, its simple beauty, its long association with weddings, the memory of family examples, and the opportunity it afforded a woman to show her mettle seem more important.

Whig's Defeat, circa 1840. McKinny, Texas, maker unknown. The high quality of design and execution suggests this quilt was made in Tennessee. *From the collection of Carolyn Roller Miller.*

Details of McKinney quilt

Detail of Northern Kentucky quilt

Whig's Defeat, circa 1890. Northern Kentucky, maker unknown. The quilt maker modified the old design and used the popular Southern color combination of the late nineteenth century, particularly in mid-South. Instead of the "feathers," she made the more familiar duck's foot to create this amusing variation. *From the collection of Gaye Rice Ingram. Photography by Kevin Beasley.*

Whig's Defeat, circa 1880. This quilt is from the estate of Lamar Polk of Alexandria, Louisiana, kinsman of James I. Polk. Note use of orange, gold, and oxblood colors used in many Southern quilts after the Civil War. *From the collection of Carolyn Roller Miller.*

Whig's Defeat, circa 1870. Provenance unknown. *From the collection of Gaye Rice Ingram. Photography by Kevin Beasley.*

Whig's Defeat, circa 1890, 62" × 98". North Carolina, maker unknown. This bold example is an unusually narrow size that features dense quilting and a zigzag border. *From the collection of Mary Kerr.*

Tennessee Beauty, circa 1852, 87" × 87". This stunning quilt was created in Davie County, North Carolina by Louisa Green Furches Etchison (1830–1911). *From the collection of the North Carolina Museum of History.*

Epilogue
Preserving Our Heritage

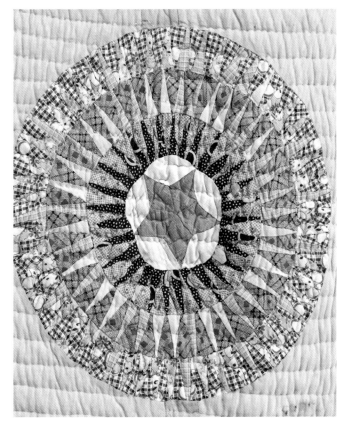

My hope with this project is that by sharing this collection of quilts we have inspired others to look at Southern quilts with fresh, appreciative eyes. We have only scratched the surface of the many facets of color, design, and inspiration we can find in our Southern heritage. I look forward to seeing what we discover next! Thank you to my fellow historians for their generous gifts of time and talent.

Thank you for allowing us to share!

Detail, Sunburst Quilt (see page 40).
From the collection of Teddy Pruett.

Detail, Tree of Paradise (see page 13).
From the collection of Sue Reich.

About the Contributors

SHERRY BURKHALTER is a quilter who lives in southeast Alabama with her college sweetheart. She enjoys all things quilts, especially the stories and history behind the quilts and their makers. She and her husband own a quilt shop and help her father on his cattle ranch.
www.quiltedcreations.net

LISA ERLANDSON is a compulsive quilt collector whose habit has led to several quilt-related specialties. She is an American Quilt Society Certified Appraiser of Quilted Textiles, lecturer, quilt show judge, teacher, and quilt historian. She also owns Le Retreat House in Gainesville, Texas. She learned to sew as a child but considered it punishment (and maybe it was). She rediscovered sewing in the mid-1980s and made her first quilt in 1991. Lisa has a Master of Arts degree in Public Communication from the University of North Texas. She taught junior high school, high school, and college before deciding to focus on the quilt world.
www.lequilts.com

LYNN LANCASTER GORGES is the owner of Historic Textiles Studio in New Bern, North Carolina. Lynn has been a textile conservator and quilt restoration specialist for more than twenty-five years. Her specialty is working on antique quilts, military uniforms and flags, and antique clothing. Over the years Lynn has given lectures at many historic sites, historical societies, quilt guilds, and museums across the Southeast. She has participated as a leader in quilt documentation days in various towns in North Carolina. Since 1992 Lynn has done extensive research on the history of the early textile mills in North Carolina, concentrating on the production of woven plaids. She is a former board member of the Costume Society of America Southeast Region, and is the North Carolina regional representative for the American Quilt Study Group. Lynn is also owner of Battleground Antiques, Inc., with her husband, William Gorges.

LAUREL HORTON has researched and made quilts since 1975. Her master's thesis at the University of North Carolina–Chapel Hill was one of the earliest studies of regional variations in American quiltmaking. She has served as the director of the South Carolina Quilt History Project and as editor of the American Quilt Study Group's journal *Uncoverings*. Horton is the author of numerous publications, including *Mary Black's Family Quilts: Memory and Meaning in Everyday Life*.

GAYE RICE INGRAM has spent a lifetime studying and observing the American South. She developed and taught courses in Southern literature and culture at Louisiana Tech University, Ruston, Louisiana, where she was an associate professor, and later, at a regional college-preparatory school. Her interest in quilts arose not in the academy, however, but from a childhood where quilts were treasured as heirlooms and evidence of women's tastes and homemaking ambitions.

MARY ELIZABETH JOHNSON is a native Alabamian with an interest in quilts and quilt history stemming from early adulthood. After graduate school at the University of Alabama, she spent several years working in Manhattan, which she refers to as her "post-graduate education." Now back in her home state, she has written some twenty books, more than half of them on the subject of quilts. She is currently wrapping up work on *Alabama Quilts: Wilderness Through World War II*, to be published by the University Press of Mississippi as part of the celebration of Alabama's bicentennial celebration.

BUNNIE JORDAN considers herself a quilter and quilt lover first. She is also an appraiser accredited through the American Society of Appraisers, a student and teacher of quilt history, and an author, curator, and researcher. Bunnie is a member of several local and national quilt groups and has served on the board of directors of the American Quilt Study Group and the Virginia Quilt Museum. Her own work has been published in several magazines and books and is in both private and corporate collections. www.bunniejordan.com

MARCIA KAYLAKIE is a quilt collector, teacher, judge, and appraiser. Her lectures and workshops feature antique and vintage quilts as she shows how American quilts reflect social, political, and economic history. She is the author of *Texas Quilts and Quilters: A Lone Star Legacy*. www.texasquiltappraiser.com

TEDDY PRUETT, Southern on both sides of the family, has been a certified quilt appraiser since 1994. She is an award-winning quilter, known for her series of "Second Hand Story" quilts made of recycled vintage items. She quilts, cares for her quilt collection, and writes from a historical home in Lake City, Florida. www.teddypruett.com

SANDRA STARLEY is a certified quilt appraiser, historian, lecturer, designer, and instructor. She maintains an extensive collection of both antique quilts and research materials and is active in the American Quilt Study Group and the Quilt Alliance. She presents trunk shows on quilt history/dating and antique quilts as material culture. She enjoys reproducing quilts from her collection, especially in small scale. She has won national awards for her antique reproductions and has been part of several traveling exhibits. http://utahquiltappraiser.blogspot.com

KATHLYN SULLIVAN, a North Carolinian for forty-five years, let her love of antique quilts lead to her involvement with documenting and writing about historic North Carolina quilts. She is coauthor of *North Carolina Quilts*, wrote the text for *Gatherings: America's Quilt Heritage*, and has written articles for many periodicals. She also served as editor of *Uncoverings*, the journal of the American Quilt Study Group. She has served as guest curator at the Gregg Museum of Art & Design at North Carolina State University, the North Carolina Museum of History, the National Quilt Museum, and other venues. A long-standing member of New Horizon Quilters, she was also a quilt appraiser, judge, and quilt collector. Now retired, she currently lives in Annapolis, Maryland.

MERIKAY WALDVOGEL is an author, curator, and quilt researcher. Codirecting the Quilts of Tennessee survey with Bets Ramsey in the 1980s sparked in Merikay a keen love for Southern quilts and quilt makers. Her writings include *Quilts of Tennessee* (1986), *Soft Covers for Hard Times* (1990), and *Southern Quilts of the Civil War* (1998). She has served on the Board of Directors of American Quilt Study Group and the Alliance for American Quilts. In 2009, she was inducted into the Quilters Hall of Fame.

SARAH BLISS WRIGHT grew up in Alabama surrounded by quilts, but it was a crazy quilt made from her late father's silk neckties that ignited a desire to add quilting to her creative pursuits. Her serious study of quilt history led to research on the American textile industry in the twentieth century and its contribution to quilting through the manufacture of cotton feedsacks. Her research was presented to the American Quilt Study Group (AQSG) and published in *Uncoverings*, the AQSG journal of quilt scholastic works. Sarah is curator for "Our Quilted Past: The Impact of the Feedsack," an exhibit of Alabama feedsack quilts and Bemis Bros. Bag Company, and she is a Road Scholar for the Alabama Humanities Foundation speaking on the subject of quilt history.

Index

MARY W. KERR is an American Quilt Society certified appraiser, author, curator, and an award-winning quilter. She was born into a family of quilters and has fond memories of growing up in Athens, Georgia. Kerr has been teaching since 1987. Her current lectures and workshops focus on quilt history and the repurposing of antique textiles into contemporary quilts. Her recent work marries her love of all things vintage with the freedom of expression that is encouraged in the art quilt community. Kerr's other books include *Twisted: Modern Quilts with a Vintage Twist* and *Recycled Hexie Quilts*, among many others. **www.marywkerr.com**